*All the Angels
in the Bible*

All the Angels in the Bible

■ ■ ■

Herbert Lockyer

HENDRICKSON
PUBLISHERS

© 1995 by Hendrickson Publishers, Inc.
P. O. Box 3473
Peabody, Massachusetts 01961–3473
All rights reserved.
Printed in the United States of America.

Softcover Edition: ISBN 1-56563-198-6

Third Printing — October 1997

Contents

Preface

This is a book of angel stories. It describes in detail angelic encounters with men and women through thousands of years—from our first parents, Adam and Eve, in the Garden of Eden, to the last words of angels spoken to the apostle John during his imprisonment on the remote island of Patmos. This is about all the angels in the Bible, their nature and their ministry. During the past fifty years in my ministry as mission executive and pastor I have spoken with many who have seen angels. Some years ago I was invited to speak through an interpreter in the morning service at the Rift Valley Academy near Nairobi, Kenya, Africa. A native Mau Mau told this story after he accepted Christ in the service:

> One dark night the men of the Mau Mau tribe were climbing the hill up to the school to capture and kill the missionary children, and fulfill one of their vows by eating a white man's brain. Suddenly men in white robes appeared all around the school, with flaming swords, and the natives ran back down the hill. Then the new Christian asked, "Who were these men; were they angels?" A missionary replied, "We do not have enough men on the staff to surround the school, and we have no flaming swords." With wide eyes the native shouted, "They were angels!"

We all agreed. There was no other explanation. During the late nineteenth century, there was very little interest in angels among Christians and church leaders in England and America. Professor Moses Stuart wrote in *Bibliotheca Sacra*, February, 1843:

Of what importance can the doctrine respecting good or evil angels be to us? We owe them, it is said, no duty or homage of worship; and as they are invisible things, if they exist at all, we can never describe with any certainty, whether or when they interpose on our behalf, or interfere for the sake of injuring us. We have, therefore, no interest in this matter.

However, with the dawning of the twentieth century, minds began to unbend and hearts began to open. During the dark days of World War I the subject of beneficial angelic activity in national life made the London newspaper headlines, with the remarkable stories told by soldiers during the retreat from the battle of Mons' (France) on August 25, 1914.

Level-headed, trustworthy men testified to the appearance of heavenly guardians on behalf of the British Army and how great relief and deliverance was provided by heavenly intervention. Without the aid of angels, it was affirmed, the British would have been annihilated by the pursuing German army. So many hospitalized British soldiers spoke of "the secret army of Mons'" that many became believers. Christians began again to embrace the doctrine of angels as not resting on conjecture but upon the testimony of God.

In 1950 my dad, Herbert Henry John Lockyer, wrote a small book on the ministry and mission of angels. As time went by, he decided to rewrite and enlarge the book. He gathered and filed new material and prepared an expanded outline. About fifteen years ago he turned the files over to me saying, "You do it, Herb."

Thanks, Dad; here it is.

My dad was born in London, England in 1886. He died in his library in our home in Colorado Springs in 1984. He once said, "I would like to die surrounded by my friends," pointing out to me his books. He had his wish. After sipping a cup of English tea, he leaned back, lifted his frail arms upward to heaven for a moment, as if he were saying, "Here I am, my Lord." The nurse checked his pulse; it was silent. We in the room felt there was an angelic presence bending low to take him home.

In preparing his material I have tried so far as possible to identify all of his quoted references, but unfortunately some sources have been lost to time. I have honored dad's choice of English spellings, such as "colour."

I wish to acknowledge the work and labor of my dad; the support of my wife angel, Ardis Arlea; my secretary, Joyce McKelvey; my research editors, James R. Edwards and Jim Hancock; my artist friends, Newt Heisley and Robert Simpich (cover); my diligent agent, William G. Gohring; my successful publisher, Stephen J. Hendrickson of Hendrickson Publishers; and all who have prayed.

Herbert Lockyer, Jr.
1995

Introduction

All the Angels in the Bible is such a delightful, inviting subject. So it is surprising how few distinct treatises there are to guide our meditation on the subject of angels. One seldom even hears a sermon on the activities of angels.

Bishop Hall, writing on the common neglect of the doctrine before us, and of his own ignorance of such a sublime theme, says:

> The good Lord forgive me for that I have suffered much to forget His Divine Presence, so the presence of His holy angels. It is, I confess, my great sin that I have filled mine eyes with other objects, and have been slack in returning praises to God, for the continual assistance of those blessed and beneficent spirits. Oh, that the dust and clay were washed out of mine eyes, that I might behold together with the presence, the numbers, the beauties and excellencies of those my ever-present guardians.

Ignorance of angels and their actions is inexcusable, seeing the Scripture speaks in no uncertain terms about them, and therefore continued disregard of them is to be deplored. The sin of worshipping the angels may have forced many in the past to the other extreme of rejecting the benefit coming to us through angels. We do not pray to them nor make them the object of our worship, but own them solely as ministers of God's providence.

No honest mind can read the Bible without coming to the conclusion that its teaching on angelology is unmistakably clear. As we are to discover, there are the faithful angels—obedient servants of God, and fallen angels—examples in their sufferings of the proper deserts of sin.

The biblical unfolding of the concept and existence of angels intensifies our admiration and adoration of the grace and government of God. He, it is, who created the angels, and knowing their essence, regimen, and offices, has informed us of their gladness in our repentance and provision for our sin. Dr. John Owen, in his exhaustive commentary on Hebrews, reminds us of the spiritual edification and comfort we derive from a study of the dignified immortals, namely, the angels of God. It is the height of ingratitude, he declares:

> . . . Not to search after what may be known of this great privilege and mercy, whereof we are made partakers in the ministry of angels. God hath neither appointed nor revealed it for nothing. He expects a revenue of praise and glory for it; and how can we bless him for it when we know nothing of it? This ministry then of angels is that which with sobriety we are in a way of duty to enquire into. Let us on this account glorify God and be thankful. Great is the privilege, manifold are the blessings and benefits that we are made partakers of, by this ministry of angels. What shall we render for them, and to them? Shall we go and bow ourselves down to the angels themselves, and pay our homage of obedience to them? They all cry out with one accord, "See you do it not; we are your fellow-servants." What shall we then do? "Why!" they say, "worship God!" Glorify and praise Him, who is the God of all angels; who sends them unto whom they minister in all that they do for us. Let us bless God, I say, for the ministry of angels.

The prevailing corruption of the scriptural concept of angels should not discourage an intelligent view of these bright, celestial ministers of God. In the infinitely wise and glorious arrangements in the kingdom of the Almighty Creator, angels have their place and should therefore be recognized in our Christian life and thought. Why recite the ancient Creed and claim to believe in "all things visible and invisible" and yet in practice give no serious thought to the reality of spiritual creatures of the invisible world? The writings of Christian antiquity carry a strong sense of the fact that angels and men make up "one single City," as Augustine expressed it. We may not feel the presence of angels, nor see them, nor hear them; nevertheless, they exist and exert their influence all the same.

> The drift of pinions would we hearken,
>   Angels at our own clay-shattered doors.
> The angels keep their ancient places:—
>   Turn but a stone and start a wing!
> 'Tis ye, 'tis your estranged faces,
>   That miss the many-splendoured thing.
>   (*The Kingdom of God*, Francis Thompson)

> Angels from friendship gather half their joy.
>   (Dr. Young)

Herbert Lockyer, Sr.
Bromley, Kent
1950

SECTION ONE

■　■　■

The Nature Of Angels

1

The Spiritual Bodies of Angels

James R. Edwards
Jamestown College

All flesh is not the same . . . there are . . . heavenly bodies and there are earthly bodies . . . a natural body . . . a spiritual body. (1 Corinthians 15:39–40, 44)

The Bible does not present a specific doctrine of angels, at least not as independent and autonomous subjects as are God, Jesus Christ, the Holy Spirit, and human beings. Always and everywhere in Scripture angels appear only in relation to God and humanity, in the role of servants. Their function as well as their glory is that of service.

In both the Old and New Testaments the root word for angel means "messenger." The Hebrew word *mal'akh* in the Old Testament and the Greek word *angelos* in the New Testament mean simply "messenger," whether human or divine. When these two words refer to messengers from God, as they frequently do, they are translated into English as "angel." Angels are hence the elect (1 Timothy 5:21) ambassadors or emissaries of God. The importance of both the Hebrew *mal'akh* and Greek *angelos* for the study of angels is that both terms describe the function or duty of angels rather than their nature. That is, the nomenclature describes an *office* rather than a nature; they tell us what angels *do* rather than what they *are*. The Bible assumes throughout that God is attended by a company or host of heavenly beings who are subordinate to Himself and who share His company and reflect His glory and majesty. But, as mentioned, the Scriptures do not discuss the sociology of these beings in and of themselves. Their existence and fellowship with the Divine is assumed and not infrequently referred to, but when reference is made to them they are presented and discussed only in relation to their function as dutiful servants of the sovereign God.

The functions of God's messengers cannot be limited to specialized categories, but rather they are presented in broad and varied auxiliary functions. In general, angels simply do God's bidding, whatever that may be. They appear as helpers and protectors to people in need, as proclaimers of news or mediators of revelations from God, and as guides and guardians. Their variety of functions can be summarized in their title of Hebrews 1:14, "ministering spirits."

A primary duty assigned to angels is the protection and guardianship of the faithful. "*The angel of the* LORD *encamps around those who fear him, and he delivers them,*" assures Psalm 34:7, and God "*Will command his angels concerning you to guard you in all your ways,*" reminds Psalm 91:11. Jesus was ministered to by angels following His temptation in the wilderness (Matthew 4:11), and in the final book of the Bible, Revelation, He assigns a greater role to angels as helpers, assistants, and servants of God than does any other book in the Bible. As mediators, angels bridge the gulf between the unseen world of the divine presence and the created world inhabited by humanity, in order to communicate God's word and will (Hebrews 2:2; Revelation 1:1). The Old Testament law itself, says Paul, was transmitted by means of angels (Galatians 3:19). It was via the angel Gabriel that Mary, the mother of our Lord, received the announcement of her impregnation by the Holy Spirit and the subsequent birth of the Messiah. Occasionally angels are spoken of as guardians who supervise individual believers (Matthew 18:10) and communities of believers (Daniel 10:13, 20; 12:1; Revelation 2:1, 8, 12, 18; 3:1, 7, 14).

As executors of the divine will, angels play certain roles closely allied with divine attributes. One instance is their role as agents of affliction in the book of Revelation, where they send plagues of God's wrath on unbelieving nations (Revelation 15–16). Similarly, angels are enlisted as warriors in the army of God to fight against the rebel hosts of the Antichrist (Revelation 12:7–9; 14:14–20).

But their purpose is not limited to auxiliary functions. Unlike human beings, angels can see God (Matthew 18:10), and their vision of God, like the beatific vision itself, leads to their praise and worship of God. Nowhere is their service of God rendered more perfectly than in their prostration and worship before the divine throne (Revelation 7:11).

The Bible does not elaborate how angels, in rendering service to the divine, accomplish their various tasks, or even how they appear. As inhabitants of the kingdom of heaven they are *spiritual beings*, but they are able to manifest themselves as active and effecting agents in the empirical world. When they do, their correspondence with the material world is more than that of an idea, an essence, or an intelligence. Sometimes the correspondence with the phenomenal world is so close as to be almost indistinguishable from it. When two angels appear in Sodom in Genesis 19:1–2, Lot greets them with customary hospitality, seemingly unaware that they are not men. Prior to the birth of Samson, his father Manoah received a visit from an angel, although " ... Manoah did not realize that it was the angel of the Lord" (Judges 13:16). Similarly, the appearance of Yahweh to Abraham at the oak of Mamre in Genesis 18:1 is such that the patriarch at first saw merely three strangers. These incidents indicate that angels can, and sometimes do, affect an extraordinary likeness to humanity, whether for the purpose of testing those to whom they appear or in order to ensure that their message and purpose will not be impeded by their otherness. This likeness is apparently present in the description of Jacob's famous wrestling match at Peniel in Genesis 32:23–32, where there is some confusion whether Jacob's opponent is a man or God. From instances such as these, and particularly from the visit of the three strangers to Abraham in Genesis 18, subsequent Jewish tradition formulated a principle of hospitality that extended into the Christian era. "Do not neglect to show hospitality," reads Hebrews 13:2, "for by this some have entertained angels without knowing it" (NASB).

In addition to their ability to assume human likeness, angels are able to affect material conditions and historical events. The legend recorded in John 5:4 (KJV) of an angel descending and troubling the water at the pool of Bethesda prior to a healing is one instance of the above. But there are also others. Twice in the Book of Acts God's angel opens prison doors (Acts 5:19; 12:7). In the second of these two episodes the angel eventually slays Herod Agrippa I for arrogating to himself the glory that was due God (Acts 12:23).

Since the Scriptural accent falls on the function of angels rather than on their specific nature, the majority of what is known about their *spiritual bodies* must be learned from inference or by way of extrapolation. There are, however, occasional passages in the Bible where the search light of a particular Biblical author alights on the subject of angels, if only momentarily. One such instance is 1 Corinthians 15, where the Apostle Paul addresses the question of the resurrection body of believers. In response to the question of how the dead are raised, the apostle alludes to the obvious hierarchy of beings among physical creatures. In descending order he lists the flesh of humans, the flesh of animals, the flesh of birds, and the flesh of fish (1 Corinthians 15:39, paraphrased). The Apostle then speaks of a heavenly counterpart to this earthly hierarchy. "There are also heavenly bodies and there are earthly bodies; but the splendor of the heavenly bodies is one kind, and the splendor of the earthly bodies is another. The sun has one kind of splendor, the moon another and the stars another; and star differs from star in splendor" (1 Corinthians 15:40–41). This leads the Apostle to the form of the resurrection body, which in verse 44 is expressly called "*a spiritual body.*" Believers, says Paul, presently partake of a physical existence as embodied souls, but in the world to come they will be embodied spirits with *spiritual bodies.* To be sure, Paul does not mention angels in this passage, nor does he allude to them, but rather to the resurrection bodies of believers; but in his appeal to the category of *spiritual bodies* characterized by light and glory and defined by form, Paul is most assuredly in the realm of angels, for this corresponds with what Scripture elsewhere implies of them. In his debate with the Sadducees over the question of the resurrection, for example, Jesus likens the resurrected state of believers to an angelic state: "For in the resurrection they neither marry, nor are given in marriage, but are as the angels of God in heaven" (Matthew 22:30 KJV; see also Mark 12:25). Luke expands this saying to include immortality: "they can no longer die; for they are like the angels. They are God's children, since they are children of the resurrection" (Luke 20:36).

At present our bodies of flesh and bones are mortal, but in the resurrection, when "this mortal has put on immortality," we will have our *spiritual bodies* like unto the angels. Spiritual bodies, glorious as they are, can only be in one place at any given moment. Only God can be in every place at any given moment in all His fullness; only God is omnipresent.

The primary description of angels in Scripture is that of "*spiritual messengers*" or "*servants of fiery flames,*" a description given in Psalm 104:4. In the original Hebrew the translation "spiritual messengers" may equally be rendered "*winds as messengers,*" and is so rendered by the Jerusalem Bible. This is due to the fact that in Hebrew the word *ruach* can mean either "*wind*" or "*spirit*"; and the word *mal'akh,* as noted earlier, can mean either "*messenger*" or "*angel.*" Context alone must determine how to render both terms. Happily for us, Psalm 104:4 is quoted in Hebrews 1:7 with reference to angels. As "*spiritual messengers,*" angels are in the service of God who is spirit (John 4:24), and they conduct their duties according to the character and intents of the Divine Spirit. The reference to their being "servants of fiery flames," although rare in Scripture, further suggests the divine imprint of their character, for frequently in Scripture God is referred to as a purging fire. Moreover, in the ancient world fire, along with earth, air, and water, was held to be one of four primal substances. The description of angels as "*servants of fire*" suggests that they belong to a genuine species of creation and are not simply emanations of the divine mind.

In close conjunction with their *spiritual nature* and embodiment is the *glory* of angels. Jesus spoke of "the Son of Man com[ing] in his glory, and all the angels with him" (Matthew 25:31; see also Luke 9:26). When Luke describes the angelic announcement of the birth of the Saviour to the shepherds in the field, he speaks of glory and light surrounding the angel visitant (Luke 2:9). The light in which angels make their appearance is not their own raiment, but their clothing from God, as it were—a clothing that Satan, who "masquerades as an angel of light,"(2 Corinthians 11:14) dons when he tempts the world.

Scripture attests to angels as visible light and visible glory, although not always in the same form. In some instances, as we have seen, an angelic appearance is so close to a human appearance as to be, at least at first sight, indistinguishable from it. But normally angels are recognized as such and evoke deep respect from humans (1 Corinthians 11:10), and not infrequently fear and terror (Isaiah 6:1–5; Luke 1:11–12; 2:9; Revelation 22:8). The appearance of angels is not limited, however, to the angelic forms that are normally recognized as such. On occasion angels appear to humanity in various natural forms. In the famous call of Moses to liberate the Israelites from bondage in Egypt, in Exodus 3:2, an angel speaks to Moses in the form of a burning bush (see also Acts 7:30, 35). Again, the angel of the Lord conducted the Israelites through the wilderness by means of a cloud (Exodus 14:19). Angels can also make their appearance in dreams, as to Joseph prior to the birth of Jesus (Matthew 1:20, 24; 2:13, 19), and in visions, as to Cornelius, the centurion (Acts 10:3). Just as there can be doubt whether an angelic appearance is actually an angel or simply a fellow human (e.g., Genesis 19:1), so there can be doubt whether one has actually experienced an angel or only seen a vision. When Peter, for instance, is released from prison by an angel, he is not sure whether he has experienced a dream or reality (Acts 12:9).

But even in these instances the Biblical writers refrain from dwelling on the *nature and essence of angels themselves.* They focus rather on the effect of the visitation on men and women. One quality often noted of angels is their strength and power. In some instances angels are explicitly identified as strong, mighty, and powerful (2 Thessalonians 1:7; 2 Peter 2:11; Revelation 5:2; 10:1; 18:21), whereas in others their might is reflected in picturesque imagery, like that of thundering waters (Revelation 16:5). Another quality, not surprisingly, is their beauty and sublimity. At the death of the first Christian martyr, we are told that the face of Stephen shone like that of an angel (Acts 6:15). The beauty need not be limited to visual beauty. It sometimes includes the beauty of angelic speech, for example—which as Paul reminds us, sublime though it is, is not a substitute for the gift of love (1 Corinthians 13:1).

Further attributes of angels appear in a series of references in the books of 1 and 2 Samuel. In a statement attesting to the moral rectitude of angels, David is said to be as "as pleasing . . . as an angel" (1 Samuel 29:9; see also 2 Samuel 19:27). David's wisdom and sense of justice are also likened to angelic wisdom and justice: " . . . the king is like an angel of God in discerning good and evil" (2 Samuel 14:17; also 14:20).

Angels are marvelous creatures, encompassed with splendor and glory; a God-given source of strength, inspiration, and encouragement to the faithful. But the Scriptures are careful to relegate angels to their rightful place in the created order and not to confuse them with God. As divine ambassadors, angels are clearly placed in the intermediate realm between God and humanity. They are not to be confused with God, for they are not eternal but created (Colossians 1:16–17). Although they are beyond human understanding (Judges 13:18), they are not omniscient. They neither know the time of the return of the Son of Man (Mark 13:32; Matthew 24:36), nor have they fully perceived the mysteries of God (1 Peter 1:12). Like all creation, angels are capable of error (Job 4:18; Psalm 78:49; 2 Peter 2:4; Jude 6). Particularly the intertestamental literature makes a great deal of the defection and fall of a particular exalted angel, to lead a subsequent revolt against the Almighty. But neither that angel nor any other is to be thought of as possessing the essence or attributes of God, or of any member of the Holy Trinity, including Jesus as the Son of God. The Son of God, according to the clear testimony of the New Testament, is both the creator of the angels' powers and virtues (Colossians 1:16–17) and their Lord—as He is of all creation, whether seen or unseen (Hebrews 1:4, 5, 6, 13; 1 Peter 3:22).

Two words remain in order, apart from which this discussion of the *spiritual bodies* of angels is not complete. The first concerns a danger inherent in the study of God's holy and elect messengers. Angels, as we have noted, are wonderful and marvelous creatures whose glory consists in their unique serviceability to the divine will. But their glory is also a possible source of error. Already in Colossians Paul speaks of a tendency among some to elevate angels and the things associated with them at the expense of Christ (Colossians 2:18). Likewise, in the Book of Revelation, which speaks of angels more often than any other book of the Bible, the Seer John had to be admonished not to worship an angelic messenger but to worship God (Revelation 19:10; 22:8–9). The tendency to be blinded by the angel rather than enlightened by its message is an ever-present threat. The fascination with angels in themselves rather than with the purpose for which they are sent is not unlike the misperception on the part of a dog that looks to the pointed finger rather than the object pointed to. The care and reserve with which the Scriptures broach the subject of angels was thrown to the wind already in the patristic period when angels began to be considered as subjects unto themselves rather than as vessels of the divine will. With the *Celestial Hierarchies* of Pseudo-Dionysus in the early Middle Ages and the full-blown treatment of angels in the scholastic period (as witnessed in Thomas Aquinas's discussions concerning their immateriality, incorruptibility, orders, ranks, telepathic communications, and relation to space and velocity), angels, whose purpose is to direct the gaze to God and lead humanity in His will, became the source of distraction from God in endless speculations. Early and ever after, in other words, believers have been tempted to shift the emphasis on angels from their office to their nature, thereby departing from the Scriptural testimony to them. When this happens, the error and loss are doubled, for angels are desecrated and humans are not led to salvation. John Calvin's sober corrective at this point, "not to speak, or guess, or even to know, concerning obscure matters anything except what has been imparted to us by God's word" (*Institutes of the Christian Religion*, I.14.4), can be as helpful in our day as it was in his.

> The name angel refers to their office, not their nature. You ask the name of their nature. It is spirit. You ask their office. It is that of an Angel, who is a messenger. (St. Augustine)

> Bright angels, by imperial summons called,
>   Innumerable before the Almighty's throne:—
> Vital in every part, not as frail man:—
>   All heart they live, all head, all eye, all ear,
> All intellect, all sense; and as they please,
>   They limb themselves, and colour, shape or size,
> Assume, as likes them best, condense, or rare. (Milton)

2

The Creation and Home of Angels

A. Their Creation

Then the LORD answered Job out of the storm. He said: ..."Where were you when I laid the earth's foundation? . . . While the morning stars sang together and all the angels shouted for joy?" (Job 38:1, 4, 7)

There is a class of beings who inhabit the expanse of the heavens. They are the angels of God; they are the tenants of the heavens. Would it be like God to have fashioned the boundless universe with no creatures to praise Him except mortal man?

The Angels are living beings of the highest position and greatest consequence in the universe. They are more than mere powers emanating from God. Though in no way independent in the sense that they are self-originating, self-sustaining, or capable of self-annihilation, they are free moral beings and, in the past ages at least, held their own destiny within the power of their own choice. (Lewis Sperry Chafer, *Systematic Theology*, VII, p. 4–5)

William George, in his *Commentary on Hebrews*, states: "Angels as first created were after the image of God: The purest, holiest and readiest to do goodness of any creatures. . . . They are the most glorious of God's creatures." Daniel described an angel as a man dressed in fine linen, with a belt of fine gold around his waist. His body was like chrysolite, his face like lightening, his eyes like flaming torches, his arms and legs of burnished bronze, and his voice like the sound of many waters (Daniel 10:5–6).

Angels have the highest habitation of all creatures: far beyond the moon and sun are all the glorious hosts of the highest visible heaven. ". . . angels in heaven always see the face of my Father in heaven" (Matthew 18:10). They have knowledge, prudence, purity, glory, power, speed, zeal and immortality.

Such is the excellence of these resplendent beings, created of a substance which is spiritual—the most excellent substance that any creature can have, and that which is nearest to the divine nature. When God spoke to Job out of the whirlwind, we find a hint as to the time when angels came into being.

Where were you when I laid the earth's foundation?
   Tell me, if you understand.
Who worked out its dimensions? Surely you know!
   Who stretched a measuring line across it?
On what was its footing set,
   Or who laid out its cornerstone—
While the mornings stars sang together
   and all the angels shouted for joy?   (Job 38:4–7)

David declares that the angels were created by God:

Praise Him, all His angels,
   Praise Him, all His heavenly hosts.
. . . for he commanded and they were created.
                              (Psalm 148:2, 5)

It is assumed from Colossians 1:16–17 that all angels were created simultaneously. In like manner, it is assumed that the creation of angels was completed at that time and that none will be added to their number. They are not subject to death or any form of extinction; therefore they do not decrease as they do not increase. The plan by which the human family is secured through propagation has no counterpart among the angels. Each angel, being a direct creation of God, stands in immediate and personal relation to the Creator. It is said by Christ, " . . . they neither marry, nor are given in marriage, but are as the angels of God in heaven" (Matthew 22:28–30, KJV). Thus it is concluded that there is no decrease or increase among these heavenly beings.

> As spirits, angels have a definite form of organization which is adapted to the law of their being. They are both finite and spacial. All this may be true though they are far removed from this mundane economy. They are able to approach the sphere of human life, but that fact in no way imposes upon them the conformity to human existence. The appearance of angels may be, as occasion demands, so like men that they pass as men. How else could some "entertain angels unawares" (Hebrews 13:2)? On the other hand, their appearance is sometimes in dazzling white and blazing glory (Matthew 28:2–4). When Christ declared, "A spirit does not have flesh and bones, as you see I have" (Luke 24:37–39), He did not imply that a spirit has no body at all, but, rather, that they do have bodies which in constitution are different from those of men. (Lewis Sperry Chafer, *Systematic Theology,* VII, p. 12)

The prophet Nehemiah writes, "You alone are the LORD. You made the heavens, . . . You give life to everything, and the multitudes of heaven worship you" (Nehemiah 9:6).

Originally, God existed alone in all the perfection and glory of His majesty. Before the appearance of any world, He surrounded Himself with a vast angelic host, spiritual beings far superior to man. Being pure spirit, the angels were and are invisible and immortal, but not immutable. When created, they were endowed with intellect, will and beauty, and power far above the human level. They all worshiped God in the excellence of His holiness, until the fall of Satan. While Scripture is sufficiently clear as to the existence of angels as creations of the Almighty, the time, order, place, and manner of the creation of the noblest and most exalted creatures of God are not revealed. Thus, opinions differ as to when and why they were brought into being.

Some Jewish writers held that they were created during the six days of creation of the world and that they are to be considered as included in the term "heaven" or "light." Rabbi Jochanan, quoting Psalm 104:3–4, affirmed that the angels were created on the second day. Rabbi Chanina, comparing Genesis 1:20 with Isaiah 40:26, says they were created on the fifth day. Another rabbi expressed the idea that only those angels created on the second day of creation continue forever. The others perish, like those created on the fifth day who sang their anthem to God's praise, then ceased to be. One Jewish writer declared, "Before the creation of the world, the blessed God created the shape of the holy angels, who were the beginning of all created beings and were derived from the glance of His glory." Another writer, misapplying Lamentations 3:23 ("They are new every morning"), remarked that "every day ministering angels are created out of the river Dinor, or 'fiery stream,' sing their anthem, then cease to exist" (Daniel 7:10). Supposedly, some angels are created from fire, others from water, others from wind. Rabbi Jochanan inferred that there is an angel created by every word that proceeds out of God's mouth.

Angels are not expressly mentioned in Moses' account of creation, yet they are implied in it. The heavens include all that are in them created by God, and among these must be the angels (Genesis 2:1). Among the hosts of heaven the angels are the principal part. They are expressly called "*the heavenly host*" and "*the armies of heaven*" (Luke 2:13). The angels must have been created with the heavens, seeing their nature is similar to the heavens and their habitation is in the heavens. It is our conviction, however, that the creation record was not designed to include a history of celestial beings, but to present a faithful account of the creation of the earth in connection with the rest of the solar system, and also of the origin and fall of man. The statement of Job indicates that the myriads of angels were created long before the creation of the world (38:4–7). With the appearance of the first and brightest productions of creative power, the holy angels—the sons of God, the morning stars of the creation—witnessed, adored and rejoiced with exultation. Angelic beings then, we confidently conclude, were created long before the formation of the earth. But just when in the mysterious revolutions of eternity they were called into existence is not a subject of divine revelation. *That* the angels were created by God and for His glory is, however, an unassailable fact of Scripture.

When created by God, all the angels were good. Some, however, fell from their celestial wisdom and position through the misuse of their liberty. God made nothing evil. The evil spirits were not created demons but became demons when by a free act they cut themselves off from their Creator. "The angels who did not keep their positions of authority but abandoned their own home—these he has kept in darkness . . . " (Jude 6). "For . . . God did not spare angels when they sinned . . . " (2 Peter 2:4). Rev. Thomas Timpson, for many years pastor of the Union Chapel, Lewisham, London, published in 1865 one of the most comprehensive studies on *The Angels of God.* On the creation of angels he has written:

> Many of the sacred writers, at least fifteen, have described these celestial beings, with the most perfect harmony of language, without a single discordant idea. Their descriptions, it may be observed, are extensively various, comprising many particulars and wholly independent of each other. All the several writers are also in this respect original. Not one is a copier, not one a plagiary; yet their representations are conversably consistent: the beings created by God are noble, sublime, dignified, beautiful, and lovely beyond anything found in the profound and finished writings of uninspired men.

> Angel spirits, by great God designed
> To be on earth the
> guardians of mankind;
> Invisible to mortal eyes they go,
> And mark our actions, good or bad below;
> The immortal eyes with watchful care preside,
> And thrice ten thousands round their charges glide.
> They can reward with glory or with gold;
> Such power Divine Permission bids them hold.
> ("Opera et Dies")

B. Their Home

And the angels who did not keep their positions of authority, but abandoned their own home . . . (Jude 6)

Angels are not always on the move; they have a natural habitat, a proper home. Is space their home? The *Judaica* teaches that there are seven heavens:

Velim—the curtain of night and day (Isaiah 40:22)
Expanse—the firmament (Genesis 1:17)
Aether—where the manna is made (Psalm 78:27)
Habitation—where Michael stands at the altar (1 Kings 8:3)
Dwelling Place—where the angels sing (Psalm 42:8)
Fixed Residence—the dwelling place (1 Kings 8:39–49)
Araboth—these are the souls of the righteous (Psalm 49:17)

The Bible mentions three heavens. "I know a man in Christ who fourteen years ago was caught up to the third heaven. Whether it was in the body or out of the body I do not know—God knows" (2 Corinthians 12:2). These words, written by Paul to the great church he founded in the thriving city of Corinth, relate to a beatific vision he had had some "fourteen years ago." This would have been some time between his conversion on the road to Damascus and his first missionary journey from Antioch.

In this vision Paul thinks of himself as passing beyond the lower sky, beyond the firmament of heaven, into a third yet higher heaven where the presence of God was manifest . . . We probably hear a far off echo of the derision with which the announcement was received by the jesting Greeks of Corinth and by St. Paul's personal rivals in the dialogue ascribed to Lucian and known as the *Pifilopatis*, in which Paul is represented as "the Galilean, bald, with eagle nose walking through the air to the third heaven" (H. E. Plumptree, *Lang's Commentary*, Vol. VII, p. 409).

Even learned Paul with his mastery of the majestic Greek language could not find words to describe the magnificence of this "*third heaven.*" He said that, to keep him from becoming conceited because of these surpassingly great revelations, " . . . there was given me a thorn in the flesh, a messenger of Satan, to torment me" (2 Corinthians 12:7). Where is the third heaven? How can we distinguish one heaven from another? Where do the angels dwell?

1. The First Heaven: Earth and Man

Then God said, "Let us make man in our image, in our likeness, and let them rule over the fish of the sea and the birds of the air, over the livestock, over all the earth . . ." (Genesis 1:26)

Earth may be miserably small, but it is our home. Here we experience change and decay, war and peace, birth and death. It is not only land and sea; there is the air we breath, the fragile atmosphere that protects us from the blazing sun and provides the rain and snow to water the earth. It is a wonderful world. "God so loved the world that He gave His one and only son . . . " (John 3:16). This world, our world of all nations, is "one precious in His sight."

Not only are we loved by God, we are ministered to by the angels. They visit us; they guide and guard us; and if we believe, they carry us into His presence.

This world is also tormented by Satan and his fallen angels. It is a world of light and darkness, of sin and salvation. As Frank Peretti states, it is a place of "present darkness." Here we take our stand against the devil's schemes, against the forces of evil in the heavenly realms. "For our struggle is not against flesh and blood, but against the rulers, against the authorities, against the powers of this dark world and against the spiritual forces of evil in the heavenly realms" (Ephesians 6:12).

A mighty fortress is our God,
A bulwark never failing;
Our helper He, amid the flood
Of mortal ills prevailing.
For still our ancient foe
Doth seek to work us woe;
His craft and power are great,
And, armed with cruel hate,
On earth is not his equal.

Did we in our own strength confide,
Our striving would be losing,
Were not the right Man on our side,

The Man of God's own choosing.
Dost ask who that may be?
Christ Jesus, it is He;
Lord Sabaoth His name,
From age to age the same,
And He must win the battle.

And though this world, with devils filled,
Should threaten to undo us,
We will not fear, for God hath willed
His truth to triumph through us.
The prince of darkness grim—
We tremble not for him;
His rage we can endure,
For lo! his doom is sure,
One little word shall fell him.

That word above all earthly powers—
No thanks to them—abideth;
The Spirit and the gifts are ours
Through Him who with us sideth.
Let goods and kindred go,
This mortal life also;
The body they may kill;
God's truth abideth still;
His kingdom is forever! (Martin Luther)

2. The Second Heaven: Space and Stars

The stars of heaven and their constellations will not show their light. The rising sun will be darkened and the moon will not give its light. (Isaiah 13:10)

The first known Christian scholar, Clement of Alexandria (155–220), who taught in the Catechetical School of Alexandria (ca. 190), believed "that the stars are angels," meaning no doubt that there are at least as many angels as there are stars. The great expanse of the universe we see on a clear star-lit night must be the second heaven.

God's throne is above the stars. "I will raise my throne above the stars . . . " (Isaiah 14:13). Stars and angels seem to go together. At the birth of Jesus the star shone and the angels sang. John in the book of Revelation writes, "the seven stars are seven angels."

> Silent, one by one in the
> infinite meadows of heaven,
> Blossomed by the lovely stars,
> the forget-me-nots of angels. (Longfellow)

It is also significant and not without meaning that the phrase "the host of heavens" means both the stars and the angelic hosts. The "Lord of Hosts" has also the same double meaning, for He is the Lord of the stars and the Lord of the angels. Our mind staggers and our heart is filled with awe as we listen to the wonders of astronomy. David said of God, "He determines the number of the stars and calls them each by name" (Psalm 147:4). Most of the names have been lost, but over 100 are preserved through the Arabic and the Hebrew and are used by astronomers today:

> We have to remember that our *written* Scriptures began with Moses, say in 1490 B.C.: and thus, for more than 2,500 years, the revelation of the hope which God gave in Genesis 3:15 was preserved in the *naming* of the stars and their *grouping* in Signs and Constellations.
>
> These groupings are quite arbitrary. There is nothing in the positions of the stars to suggest the pictures originally drawn around them. The Signs and Constellations were first designed and named; then, the pictures were drawn around them respectively. Thus the truth was enshrined and written in the heavens, where no human hand could touch it. In later years, when Israel came into the possession of the written "Scriptures of truth," there was no longer any need for the more ancient writing in the heavens. Hence, the original teaching gradually faded away, and the heathen, out of the smattering they had heard by tradition, evolved their cosmogonies and mythologies. (*Companion Bible*, Part 1, Note 12)

In his book on stars astronomer Jay M. Pasachoft writes, "Light travels at 186,000 miles per second. . . . Light can travel the distance around the earth in a simple second . . . can travel from the sun in eight minutes. Yet it takes four years to travel from the nearest stars." (*Guide to the Stars*, p. 110). Job mentions the star Arcturas (Job 9:9 KJV). This star is thirty-six light years from the earth, which is 351,941,760,000 miles from the earth; yet we can see it, for it is twenty-five times the diameter of the sun. Camille Flammarion states:

> Then I understand that all the stars which have ever been observed in the sky, the millions of luminous points which constitute the Milky Way, the innumerable celestial bodies, suns of every magnitude and of every degree of brightness, solar systems, planets and satellites, which by millions and hundreds of millions succeed each other in the void around us, that whatever human tongues have designated by the name of universe, do not in the infinite represent more than an archipelago of celestial islands and not more than a city in a grand total of population, a town of greater or lesser importance. In this city of the limitless empire, in this town of a land without frontiers, our Sun and its system represents a single point, a single house among millions of other habitations. Is our solar system a palace or a hovel in this great city? Probably a hovel. And the earth? The Earth is a room in the solar mansion—a small dwelling, miserably small. (cited by Gaebelein, "The Angels of God," pp. 8–9)

From earliest times man has asked the question, "Is Earth the only inhabited planet?" The Bible, addressing this age-old problem, discloses that the angels have their abode among the stars, in the heavens—the second heaven. Their numbers are beyond human computation.

3. The Third Heaven: God and Glory

I know a man in Christ [Paul] who . . . was caught up to the third heaven. (2 Corinthians 12:2)

This is the place of divine glory, the place of the blessed, seen by Moses, Ezekiel, Paul, John and Satan. "*One day the angels came to present themselves before the* LORD, *and Satan also came with them. The* LORD *said to Satan, 'Where have you come from?' Satan answered the* LORD, *'From roaming through the earth and going back and forth in it'"* (Job 1:6).

Dr. A. Gaebelein, in his book *Angels,* states:

In the Hebrew, heaven is the plural, "the heavens." The Bible speaks of three heavens, the third heaven is the heaven of heavens, the dwelling place of God, where His throne has always been. The tabernacle possessed by His earthly people, Israel, was a pattern of the heavens. Moses upon the mountain had looked into the vast heavens and saw the three heavens. He had no telescope. But God Himself showed to him the mysteries of the heavens. Then God admonished him when he was about to make tabernacle and said to His servant, "See that thou make all things according to the pattern showed to thee in the mountain" (Hebrews viii:5). The tabernacle had three compartments, the outer court, the Holy part and the Holiest. Once a year the high priest entered this earthly place of worship to pass through the outer court, into the Holy part, and, finally, carrying the sacrificial blood, he entered into the Holiest to sprinkle the blood in Jehovah's holy presence. But Aaron was only a type of Him who is greater than Aaron, the true High Priest. Of Him, the true Priest, our Lord and Saviour Jesus Christ, it is written that He passed *through the heavens* (Hebrews iv:14). "For Christ is not entered into the holy places made with hands, which are the figures of the true, but into heaven itself, now to appear in the presence of God for us" (Hebrews ix:24). He passed through the heavens, the outer court, the heaven surrounding the earth; the holy part, the immense universes, with their immeasurable distance, and finally He entered the third heaven, that heaven astronomy knows exists, but which no telescope can ever reach.

The glory and majesty of God in the highest heaven was seen by the following people:

Moses, as he with the elders went up Mt. Sinai, saw during his six days " . . . the God of Israel. Under his feet was something like a pavement made of sapphire, clear as the sky itself" (Exodus 24:9,10).

Ezekiel saw "what looked like a throne of sapphire, and high above on the throne was a figure like that of a man . . . as if full of fire . . . and brilliant light surrounded him" (Ezekiel 1:26–27).

John, as he prayed in his cave on the Isle of Patmos, exclaimed, ". . . I was in the Spirit, and there before me was a throne in heaven with someone sitting on it. And the one who sat there had the appearance of jasper . . . " (Revelation 4:2).

This dwelling place of the Most High, the third heaven, referred to by Paul (2 Corinthians 12:2) is the highest heaven. The faithful angels can go in a moment from their abode in the second heaven into the presence of God, their Creator, in the third heaven to praise Him and to obey His command to visit the dusty lanes of earth of the first heaven, to guard the people of the Way, to watch over our little children and to execute judgment on the wicked.

> Beyond the glittering starry globes,
> Far as the eternal hills,
> There all the boundless worlds, with light,
> Our great Redeemer fills.

> Legions of Angels, strong and fair,
> In countless armies shine;
> And swell his praise with golden harps,
> Attuned to songs divine. (Gregg)

3

The Number of Angels

As I looked, thrones were set in place, and the Ancient of Days took his seat. His clothing was as white as snow; the hair of his head was white like wool. His throne was flaming with fire, and its wheels were all ablaze. A river of fire was flowing, coming out from before him. Thousands upon thousands attended him; ten thousand times ten thousand stood before him. The court was seated, and the books were opened. (Daniel 7:9–10)

The great hosts of angels were created at one time. Scripture informs us that their number is "legion." The ancients believed they spoke Hebrew and thus only prayers in Hebrew would be heard by the angels. According to the words of our Lord in Matthew 22:30 ("At the resurrection people will neither marry nor be given in marriage; they will be like the angels in heaven"), the angels do not multiply as does the human race. There are children in heaven—our children—but there are no baby angels.

The Scriptures are silent as to the exact number of angels, but with no uncertain voice they declare that the angels are counted in the millions. Thomas Aquinas, early church father and theologian, assigned one angel to every human on earth, and that would mean today their number is 5.5 billion. Scripture teaches that the angels are as multitudinous as the stars. In Genesis 28:12 and 32:1, we read how Jacob saw the angels of God ascending and descending a ladder that reached up to heaven. The angels were his companions and protection. When the patriarch returned home he called the name of the place *Mahanaim*, which means "two camps of armies." Moses wrote, "The Lord came from Sinai . . . He came with myriads of holy ones . . ."

(Deuteronomy 33:2). David said in Psalm 148, "Praise him, all his angels, praise him all his heavenly hosts," and also in Psalm 103:21, "Praise the Lord, all his heavenly hosts . . . ." Micaiah the prophet said, "I saw the Lord sitting on his throne with all the hosts of heaven standing around him . . ." (1 Kings 22:19). Daniel in his vision of God said, "Thousands upon thousands attended him; ten thousand times ten thousand stood before him" (Daniel 7:10).

The Lord Jesus in Matthew 26:52 said to Peter, "Do you think that I cannot call on my Father, and He will at once put at my disposal more than twelve legion of angels?" The Roman legion was composed of 6,200 foot soldiers and 300 horse soldiers; thus 12 legions would be 78,000 men—or angels. The demon-possessed man in Mark 5:9 said, "My name is Legion, . . . for we are many." A legion is a term for many. Our Lord's usage of the word "legion" implied an unnumbered army of angels were at His command.

In Hebrews we have this beautiful expression: "But you have come to Mount Zion, to the heavenly Jerusalem, the city of the living God. You have come to thousands upon thousands of angels in joyful assembly . . ." (Hebrews 12:22). The apostle John in the book of Revelation, describing the heavenly hosts, used words similar to those of the writer of Hebrews: "Then I looked and heard the voice of many angels, numbering thousands upon thousands, and ten thousand times ten thousand. . . . In a loud voice they sang: 'Worthy is the Lamb . . .' " (Revelation 5:11–12). The number of angels worshipping round about the throne was one hundred million to begin with, then millions upon millions. Their numbers are symbolic of a numberless throng which raised their song.

> Divine Revelation was designed to afford us information on many points relating to the government of God, both in heaven and on earth; but chiefly to make us wise unto salvation, through faith in Christ Jesus. We ought not, therefore, to expect that it would make us perfectly acquainted with the whole economy of the celestial world: still the instruction given to us in the Scriptures regarding angelic spirits is extensive; calculated to awaken in us a spirit of enquiry, and to lead us to aspire after conformity to them in holiness, that we may be qualified to enjoy their society, and unite

with them in acts of worship before the throne of our glorious Creator. At present we are unable to ascertain their appropriate rank and stations, or their incalculable numbers. (Thomas Timpson, *Angels*)

4

The Names and Titles of Angels

For by him all thing were created: things in heaven and on earth, visible and invisible, whether thrones or powers or rulers or authorities; all things were created by him and for him. (Colossians 1:16)

Then Manoah inquired of the angel of the LORD, "What is your name, so that we may honor you when your word comes true?" He replied, "Why do you ask my name? It is beyond understanding." (Judges 13:17–18)

A. Introduction

Angels being of a nature so excellent and filling offices so exalted as we find in the kingdom of God, we might rationally expect that they would be described under names and titles corresponding to their dignified stations. Such, we perceive, is the case, both in the Old and the New Testament. Although the Bible does not give us a complete unfolding of the ranks and stations of heaven's most dignified intelligent creatures, enough can be gathered from their honourable names and titles to prove that there were certain orders, classes or grades among the angelic hierarchy.

Significant and expressive as the terms here employed may be regarded, they appear peculiarly appropriate; and there are several others, still more expressive, employed to designate angels as they are found in different parts of the Bible. Our inquiries must, therefore, include all these titles; that we may be the better prepared to form correct and worthy conceptions of these glorious creatures of our God and Saviour.

B. Angels

"Angels" are mentioned in thirty-four different books of the Bible. The word "angel," in its singular, possessive and plural cases, appears 305 times in the Bible (NIV—See Bible references in Compendium). The word "angel" implies "I dispatch, I send." Angels are, therefore, so called not to indicate their nature, but simply to designate their official character. In a very special manner, they are employed in numberless ways as the messengers of God, to saved and sinners alike. Bishop G. M. Hopkins calls the angels "glorious spirits, the top and cream of creation. They are always *spirits,* but when they are sent they are called *Angels.*"

> Do you enquire the name of their nature?—It is spirit.
> Do you ask the name of their service?—It is angel. (St. Augustine)

The Bible applies the word "angel" in various ways. First: It is used of God. "The Angel of God" or "Jehovah" usually signifies a theophanic appearance of Christ (a pre-incarnation appearance of Christ in the Old Testament)—the presence of Deity in angelic form (Genesis 16:7,9, 10; 22:11; Zechariah 1:11). (This we discuss in the chapter, "The Angel of the Covenant.")

Second: It is used of men. The words "angels" and "messengers," as we have seen, are equivalents, as passages like Genesis 32:3; Deuteronomy 2:26; Malachi 3:1; Luke 7:24; 9:52 and Revelation 22:16 clearly prove. The original word is also used to describe God's created messengers, such as:

Israel (Isaiah 42:19)
Haggai (Haggai 1:13)
John the Baptist (Malachi 2:7; 3:1)
The Priesthood (Ecclesiastes 5:6)
Pastors or Bishops of the Church (Revelation 1:20)

Third: It is used of celestial beings. In the majority of cases "angel," in the Bible, is used of the unseen hierarchy of heaven, each with his particular office to fulfill and talent to use, and all employed in numberless ways as the messengers of God to needy men. The faithful angels are pure spirits and assume corporeal forms only on particular occasions. The Bible alone supplies us with an authentic revelation of the existence and nature of angels, described, as we now see, in many characteristic ways.

1. Gabriel

> The angel answered, "I am Gabriel. I stand in the presence of God, and I have been sent to speak to you and to tell you this good news." (Luke 1:19)

The name of this principal angel means "*the strength of God.*" Gabriel was employed on several important missions. He is not mentioned as having contact with the devil. He seems to be the angelic prophet, an interpreter of the prophetic Word, and a revealer of the purposes of God. It was Gabriel who flew swiftly to Daniel to inform him and to give him skill and understanding of things to come. He expounded to the prophet the whole course of Gentile history (Daniel 8:16–27; 9:21). It was Gabriel who revealed to Zechariah that he was to be the father of John, the forerunner of Christ (Luke 1:19). It was Gabriel who revealed to Mary that she was to be the virgin mother of the Saviour of mankind (Luke 1:26–35).

Bible References to the Angel Gabriel:

> And I heard a man's voice from the Ulai calling, "Gabriel, tell this man the meaning of the vision." (Daniel 8:16)

> . . . while I was still in prayer, Gabriel, the man I had seen in the earlier vision, came to me in swift flight about the time of the evening sacrifice. (Daniel 9:21)

> The angel answered, "I am Gabriel. I stand in the presence of God, and I have been sent to speak to you and to tell you this good news. . . ." (Luke 1:19)

> In the sixth month, God sent the angel Gabriel to Nazareth, a town in Galilee. . . . (Luke 1:26)

2. Michael

But even the archangel Michael, when he was disputing with the devil about the body of Moses, did not dare to bring a slanderous accusation against him, but said, "The Lord rebuke you!" (Jude 9)

Michael is the only angel to be named "The Archangel." We are not told who the archangel is whose voice will be heard at the resurrection of the dead in Christ (1 Thessalonians 4:16). The Apocrypha names several archangels who present the prayers of saints, and who go constantly in and out of the presence of God. Because of his prominent tasks Michael can be classed among the chief angels.

Michael means "*who is like unto God,*" a name of self-oblation, of self-obliteration. He did not glorify himself. In the Book of Enoch his meekness is extolled: "the merciful, the patient, the holy Michael." Some writers have identified this angel of great dignity and glory in the court of heaven as Christ the Messiah. This theory is to be rejected, however, seeing Daniel calls Michael one of the chief or capital princes (Daniel 10:13; 12:1). In the Old Testament he appears as the guardian or patron angel of Daniel and of the people of Israel. In the New Testament he is mentioned by Jude (verse 9) as contending with the devil and by John as the archangel victorious over the archenemy, the dragon (Revelation 12:7). Michael overcame the evil Satanic prince of Persia, who hindered Gabriel's visit to Daniel, and it will be Michael and his great celestial, militant host who will successfully war against the devil and his angels. In 1 Thessalonians 4:16 the dead will be raised and the church caught up at the "*voice of the archangel*"—it must be Michael.

Bible References to the Archangel Michael:

But the prince of the Persian kingdom resisted me twenty-one days. Then Michael, one of the chief princes, came to help me, because I was detained there with the king of Persia. (Daniel 10:13)

But first I will tell you what is written in the Book of Truth. (No one supports me against them except Michael, your prince. . . .) (Daniel 10:21)

"At that time Michael, the great prince who protects your people, will arise. There will be a time of distress such as has not happened from the beginning of nations until then. But at that time your people—everyone whose name is found written in the book—will be delivered. (Daniel 12:1)

But even the archangel Michael, when he was disputing with the devil about the body of Moses, did not dare to bring a slanderous accusation against him, but said, "The Lord rebuke you!" (Jude 9)

And there was war in heaven. Michael and his angels fought against the dragon, and the dragon and his angels fought back. (Revelation 12:7)

C. Seraphim

Then flew one of the seraphims unto me, having a live coal in his hand, which he had taken with the tongs from off the altar: And he laid it upon my mouth, and said, Lo, this hath touched thy lips: and thine iniquity is taken away, and thy sin purged." (Isaiah 6:6–7, KJV)

Seraphim (Hebrew, "burning ones") is a title given to angels by Isaiah (6:2–6). This plural word is from *seraph*, which signifies *fiery*, or *burning*. This is also the word used to describe the fiery serpents, by which the children of Israel were bitten in the wilderness of Arabia (Numbers 21:6). Some suppose that this name was given to a class of the angels on account of their missions to execute on the wicked the fiery indignation of God. But others think that they are so called from their ardent zeal for the honour and glory of their Creator, as represented in the vision of the prophet Isaiah. Indicative of purity and zeal, the seraphim are thought to be the highest order of angelic beings—inflamed by love for God because of their nearness to Him.

The seraphim are to be distinguished from the cherubim in that the former are represented as having six wings, and the latter four wings. While there are seventy-three references to the cherubim, the seraphim are only mentioned twice in Scripture. " . . . I saw the Lord seated on a throne. . . . Above him were seraphs, each with six wings: . . . Then one of the seraphs flew to me with a live coal in his hand. . . . With it he touched my mouth and said, 'Your guilt is taken away and your sins atoned for.'" (Isaiah 6:1, 2, 6–7) How significant is the description given of the Seraphim! Each seraph has six wings used in a threefold way (Isaiah 6:2).

One: *With two he covered his face.* The veiled face indicates unworthiness and also inability to steadfastly behold or fully comprehend the glory of the Lord. It also suggests profound reverence and adoring awe, as well as care not to pry into God's secrets and counsels (Exodus 3:6; Job 4:18; 15:15; 1 Kings 19:13).

Two: *With two he covered his feet.* Service consists in reverent waiting on, more than in active service for, God. Covered feet denote deep humility.

Three: *With two he did fly.* Two wings alone of the six were kept ready for instant flight. Here we have prompt celerity and alacrity in executing the will of God. Four wings were for *worship*—two wings for *work*. We are guilty of reversing the order and serve more than wait.

Then the prophet Isaiah describes the offices of the Seraphim he saw in his vision: First of all, they praise God for His holiness: "Holy, holy, holy is the Lord of Hosts . . ." (Isaiah 6:3). The most glowing of the angelic orders, glowing with the holy flame of Divine love, they are depicted as *standing* as they celebrated God's holiness and waited to execute His mandates. The threefold repetition of "Holy" has justly been thought to refer to the three divine persons in the Trinity and to the holiness displayed in the great work of redemption. It is also suggested that the epithet thrice repeated may refer to the three worlds: 1. Holy is Jehovah in the world of angels and spirits. 2. Holy is Jehovah in the middle world of stars and other heavenly bodies. 3. Holy is Jehovah upon the earth, which is His.

The seraphim are God's agents for the purification of His people. Isaiah, after pronouncing woes on others, perceived himself liable to the same condemnation. The uncleanness of his lips was in contrast to the seraphim chanting in alternate responses, with pure lips. But God encouraged the prophet, made conscious of his own sinfulness by a symbolical action of a seraph. The live coal from the altar represents the sacrifice of Christ and its effects; and, applied to the prophet's lips, denotes the assurance of pardon and acceptance in his work, through the atonement of the promised Messiah. Isaiah's unfitness for the office, as well as his personal sin, were removed only by being brought into contact with the sacrificial altar (Isaiah 6:7). Note that Satan, before he became Satan, was the highest of the seraphim. The seraphim are among the great "mysteries" we will not fully understand until we get to heaven.

Bible References to the Seraphim (Seraph):

Above him were seraphs, each with six wings: With two wings they covered their faces, with two they covered their feet, and with two they were flying. (Isaiah 6:2)

Then one of the seraphs flew to me with a live coal in his hand, which he had taken with tongs from the altar. (Isaiah 6:6)

D. Cherubim

And make two cherubim out of hammered gold at the ends of the cover. Make one cherub on one end and the second cherub on the other; make the cherubim of one piece with the cover, at the two ends. The cherubim are to have their wings spread upward, overshadowing the cover with them. The cherubim are to face each other, looking toward the cover. (Exodus 25:18–20)

Before considering the attributes and activities of the cherubim, the singular of which is cherub, it may be found profitable to discuss the distinctions between the cherubim and the seraphim. The Bible makes it clear that these two types of angelic beings represent two different orders or ranks.

The propriety of the distinction of wings must be observed. The seraphim of Isaiah have two more wings than the cherubim of Ezekiel (1:5–18; 10:12). The former are described as being more immediately before the presence of God, therefore each seraph has two wings to cover his face before such transcendent brightness. Another difference is that the seraphim sing the praises of God without intermission. Further, the seraphim, the glorious ministers of God, are from their nature compared to fire and light. Cherubim, on the other hand, are so named because of their speed in the accomplishment of their tasks. The two names are not attached to the same order of angels, even though both orders are near to God and possess the same glorious effulgence of their celestial nature.

The form and design of cherubic figures indicate immediate service for the Creator and constant attendance upon the *Shechinah*. The actual existence of the cherubim cannot be disputed. However, the cherub is used in a symbolic sense by the Psalmist when he speaks of the God of Israel riding upon a cherub (Psalm 18:10). Here the cherub appears as a personification of the storm-cloud, bearing God from heaven to earth.

The word "cherubim" means to till or plough and is expressive of diligent service. The first Biblical reference to the cherubim is in association with the expulsion of Adam and Eve from the garden of Eden (Genesis 3:24). God placed them on the east side of the garden to preserve the way to the tree of life. They guard it not against, but for man, till man shall be fit to enjoy it and never to lose it (Revelation 2:7). "Blessed are those who wash their robes, that they may have the right to the tree of life and may go through the gates into the city" (Revelation 22:14).

Moses does not specify the form of these angelic agents of divine judgment and mercy. Yet he must have been familiar with them for, when ordered to make the cherubim for the tabernacle, he fashioned them without any special direction from God. Placed at each end of the mercy seat, the cherubim represent a new relationship to God in His holiness and life-imparting presence (Exodus 25:18–20; Psalm 80:1). Their outstretched wings touch each other; they gaze one towards another, and downwards upon the ark. The position and attitude of the cherubim upon the mercy seat indicate their attendance upon their Creator and our Redeemer. Their gaze downwards upon the ark suggests their contemplation of the sublime mysteries of the Gospel: "angels long to look into these things" (1 Peter 1:12). God is said to "sit enthroned between the cherubim" (Psalm 80:1), on the mercy seat (Exodus 25:18–23), from which He promised to commune with Moses; and thus on "the throne of grace," which the redeemed are exhorted to approach boldly (Hebrews 4:16).

The cherubim made for Solomon's magnificent temple were of a colossal size (1 Kings 6:23–29) and were different from the cherubim constructed by Moses, which were made of solid gold. In the most holy place of the temple there were four cherubim, compared with the two Moses used. In Ezekiel the Cherubim are instilled for the first time with life, zeal, and ceaseless untiring motion. Thirty times they are called "the living creatures," full of the life of God, which flows everlastingly into them (Ezekiel 1:10; 10:12). In Ezekiel 1:10 and Revelation 4:7 the cherubim are called "living creatures," and in Ezekiel each one had four faces. In Revelation each one had a different face representing (1) the lion, (2) the ox, (3) the eagle and (4) the man.

What does this mean? The composite animal forms are ideal representatives of redeemed creaturely life, in which man is prominent (Ezekiel 1:5; Revelation 4:7). The *lion*, king of wild animals, signifies undaunted courage and vigour in the execution of God's commands. The *ox*, king of dumb creation, symbolizes unwearied patience and firmness. The *eagle*, king of feathered creation, represents activity, and the incomparable speed with which these celestial beings execute their divine missions. The *man*, king of God's earthly creation, speaks of prudence and compassion, intelligence and strength of reason. Man, head of all, whose ideal was realized by the Son of Man, combines all animal excellencies.

The church Fathers associated the four faces of the cherubim with the four Gospels, and the four profiles of Christ they present: *Matthew*, the *lion*: the kingly aspect of Christ's manifestation and ministry appear in this Gospel. *Mark*, the *ox*: the patience and laborious endurance of Christ are evident in this Gospel. *Luke, man*: the humaneness and brotherly sympathy are traits of Christ which Luke stresses. *John, the eagle*: the soaring majesty of the Divine Word is before us in the fourth Gospel. The fourfold face of the cherubim can also be applied to the Church of the redeemed. As the cherubim were of one piece with the Ark, so the redeemed are one with Christ, and one with Him as their propitiation (2 Peter 1:3–4; Hebrews 2:11; Exodus 29:42–46; 25:22; 1 Corinthians 3:16, 17; Gal. 2:20). In the book of Revelation the four living creatures—not beasts—are identified with the redeemed of God. The living creatures reveal who and what they are; they sing the song of redeeming grace (Revelation 5:7–8).

Bible References to the Cherubim (Cherub):

After he drove the man out, he placed on the east side of the Garden of Eden cherubim and a flaming sword flashing back and forth to guard the way to the tree of life. (Genesis 3:24)

And make two cherubim out of hammered gold at the ends of the cover. Make one cherub on one end and the second cherub on the other; make the cherubim of one piece with the cover, at the two ends. The cherubim are to have their wings spread upward, overshadowing the cover with them. The cherubim are to face each other, looking toward the cover. (Exodus 25:18–20)

There, above the cover between the two cherubim that are over the ark of the Testimony, I will meet with you and give you all my commands for the Israelites. (Exodus 25:22)

So the people sent men to Shiloh, and they brought back the ark of the covenant of the Lord Almighty, who is enthroned between the cherubim. And Eli's two sons, Hophni and Phinehas, were there with the ark of the covenant of God. (1 Samuel 4:4)

He and all his men set out from Baalah of Judah to bring from there the ark of God, which is called by the Name, the name of the Lord Almighty, who is enthroned between the cherubim that are on the ark. (2 Samuel 6:2)

He mounted the cherubim and flew; he soared on the wings of the wind. (2 Samuel 22:11)

In the inner sanctuary he made a pair of cherubim of olive wood, each ten cubits high. One wing of the first cherub was five cubits long, and the other wing five cubits—ten cubits from wing tip to wing tip. The second cherub also measured ten cubits, for the two cherubim were identical in size and shape. The height of each cherub was ten cubits. He placed the cherubim inside the innermost room of the temple, with their wings spread out. The wing of one cherub touched one wall, while the wing of the other touched the other wall, and their wings touched each other in the middle of the room. He overlaid the cherubim with gold. (1 Kings 6:23–28)

On the walls all around the temple, in both the inner and outer rooms, he carved cherubim, palm trees and open flowers. (1 Kings 6:29)

And on the two olive wood doors he carved cherubim, palm trees and open flowers, and overlaid the cherubim and palm trees with beaten gold. (1 Kings 6:32)

He carved cherubim, palm trees and open flowers on them and overlaid them with gold hammered evenly over the carvings. (1 Kings 6:35)

And Hezekiah prayed to the Lord: "O Lord, God of Israel, enthroned between the cherubim, you alone are God over all the kingdoms of the earth. You have made heaven and earth." (2 Kings 19:15)

David and all the Israelites with him went to Baalah of Judah (Kiriath Jearim) to bring up from there the ark of God the Lord, who is enthroned between the cherubim—the ark that is called by the Name. (1 Chronicles 13:6)

He mounted the cherubim and flew; he soared on the wings of the wind. (Psalm 18:10)

Hear us, O Shepherd of Israel, you who lead Joseph like a flock; you who sit enthroned between the cherubim, shine forth. (Psalm 80:1)

The Lord reigns, let the nations tremble; he sits enthroned between the cherubim, let the earth shake. (Psalm 99:1)

O Lord Almighty, God of Israel, enthroned between the cherubim, you alone are God over all the kingdoms of the earth. You have made heaven and earth. (Isaiah 37:16)

I looked, and I saw the likeness of a throne of sapphire above the expanse that was over the heads of the cherubim. (Ezekiel 10:1)

You were anointed as a guardian cherub, for so I ordained you. You were on the holy mount of God; you walked among the fiery stones. (Ezekiel 28:14)

E. Sons Of God

... the sons of God saw ... the daughters of men... (Genesis 6:2).

God presides in the great assembly; he gives judgment among the "gods" (Psalm 82:1)

I said, 'you are "gods," you are all sons of the Most High.' (Psalm 82:6)

In the council of the holy ones God is greatly feared. . . (Psalm 89:7)

He said, "Look! I see four men walking around in the fire, unbound and unharmed, and the fourth looks like a son of the gods." (Daniel 3:25)

Angels are called *sons of God* to indicate their near relationship to their Creator and also their interest in His parental care for all creation. They have power and authority as designated administrators of the divine government. They execute justice and provide protection throughout the world. Rev. John Wesley, impressed with the divine power and intelligence of the sons of God, remarks:

And what an inconceivable degree of wisdom must they have acquired, by the use of their amazing faculties, over and above that with which they were originally endowed, in the course of more than six thousand years! How immense must be their wisdom, increased during so long a period, not only by surveying the hearts and ways of men, but by observing the work of God, his works of creation, his providence, his work of Grace. And above all, by continually beholding the face of their Father in heaven. (*Wesley's Sermons,* Sermon No. 77)

F. Morning Stars

Where were you when I laid the earth's foundation . . . while the morning stars sang together and all the angels shouted for joy? (Job 38:4, 7)

Morning stars is a title given to angels, indicating their intelligence, holiness and brightness of glory; excellencies which have all been derived from their infinitely-glorious Creator. Satan was one of the morning stars (Isaiah 14:12).

G. Watchers

It is Daniel who gives angels the title of watchers.

"I saw in the visions of my head upon my bed, and, behold, a watcher and an holy one came down from heaven; . . . This matter is by the decree of the watchers, and the demand by the word of the holy ones: to the intent that the living may know that the most High ruleth in the kingdom of men, . . . And whereas the king saw a watcher and an holy one coming down from heaven . . ." (Daniel 4:13, 17, 23 KJV)

As *watchers* the angels have ever-wakeful diligence in duty. Having no need of sleep, they are untiringly active in administering their appointed affairs under God's directions. What watchful care they exercise over the saints of God, in all the toils and trials of their earthly pilgrimage! They are like the watchmen posted on the walls of Jerusalem who never sleep and are active day and night (Isaiah 62:6).

H. Thrones, Powers, Rulers, Authorities

For by him were all things created . . . whether thrones or powers or rulers or authorities. . . (Colossians 1:16)

Christ ... in the heavenly realms, far above all rule and authority, power and dominion, and every title that can be given. . . (Ephesians 1:20, 21)

"We do not know what all these titles mean. Whatever they mean, if anything, all are infinitely below the glory of Christ" (*Lang's Commentary*, volume 7, page 101). Scholar Louis Berkhof believes, "These appellations do not point to different kinds of angels, but simply to differences in rank." "These terms are applied to angels on account of their dignity as appointed rulers under the Divine Administration" (Thomas Timpson).

I. Conclusion

In the Bible four angels are mentioned by name: *Michael* is mentioned five times (Daniel 10:13; 10:21; 12:1; Jude 9, Revelation 12:7). He is the only angel to be called an archangel (Jude 9). *Gabriel* is mentioned four times (Daniel 8:15–27; 9:20–27; Luke 1:11–19, 26–27). *Lucifer* is mentioned once by name (Isaiah 14:12 KJV [Morning Star NIV]); Satan's name is mentioned 54 times. *The Angel of the Covenant (Lord)* is mentioned many times in Scriptures and is dealt with in the Chapter, "The Angel of the Covenant."

The apocryphal books mention by name the angels Metatron, Raphael, and Uriel or Jeremiel. Reviewing the preceding examination of the names and titles of angels, we perceive that they indicate their high importance as the creatures of God and are designed for our practical improvement. Those titles, the most significant that could be found in human language, may, however, but improperly describe their high distinction among created intelligences. Still it is evident that angels possess preeminent dignity in the universal kingdom of the Most High; especially their names are given to them by the infinite wisdom of God. We cannot, therefore, worthily honour His holy Word, justify our own profession of faith, or receive the full amount of the consolation designed by the Scriptures unless we give attention to the divine testimony concerning those holy, happy, and immortal beings, all of whom bear a commission of grace in our favour and are sent to serve those who will inherit salvation (Hebrews 1:14).

The following lists show some of the variety of opinion over the centuries about the ordering of the angelic hierarchy:

Gregory the Great (AD 540)	Thomas Aquinas (AD 1224)
1. Seraphim	1. Seraphim
2. Cherubim	2. Cherubim
3. Thrones	3. Thrones (Wheels)
4. Dominations	4. Dominations (Dominions)
5. Principalities	5. Virtues
6. Powers	6. Powers
7. Virtues	7. Principalities
8. Archangels	
9. Angels	

Billy Graham (*Angels*)	Our Listing
1. Archangels	1. Angels
2. Angels	2. Gabriel
3. Seraphim	3. Michael
4. Cherubim	4. Seraphim
5. Principalities	5. Cherubim
6. Authorities	6. Sons of God
7. Powers	7. Morning Stars
8. Thrones	8. Watchers
9. Might	9. Thrones
10. Dominion	10. Powers
	11. Rulers
	12. Authorities

5

The Fall of Angels

... God did not spare angels when they sinned, but sent them to hell, putting them into gloomy dungeons to be held for judgment. (2 Peter 2:4)

And the angels who did not keep their positions of authority but abandoned their own home—these he has kept in darkness, bound with everlasting chains for judgment on the great Day. (Jude 6)

A. Introduction

It seems almost inconceivable that any so highly privileged as to live so near to the throne of God, beholding and bathing in His glory, should sin against Him and consequently suffer expulsion from His presence. But such was the case, and Scripture is not silent as to open rebellion in the angelic hierarchy.

Without doubt, the vast majority of the celestial cohorts have been true to God since their creation. They never cease to do His will in heaven. They have never defaulted, have ever been ready to run His errands. These are the angels who excel in strength and who, as God's ministers, do His commandments and hearken to the voice of His word. "Praise the Lord, you his angels, you mighty ones who do his bidding, who obey his word. Praise the Lord, all his heavenly hosts, you his servants who do his will" (Psalm 103:20–21).

In this section of our study we are to discover what the Bible says about the fallen in God's angelic family—the angels God charges with folly (Job 4:18). The assertion of Job proves that the angels were capable of committing sin, which was precisely what the fallen angels did. They were not so intelligent as to be incapable of the most egregious folly if a work like that of governing the world were entrusted to them for one single hour. God, therefore, can put no trust in them; and He charges even them with folly.

Before discovering what the Bible teaches about the fallen angels we need to consider the highest angelic being responsible for the angels' rebellion against God. It is evident that *Satan* is the monarch of the fallen angels, for our Lord speaks of "the devil and his angels." Revelation, reason, and experience warn us that there is a spiritual intelligence abroad in the world which is malignant and ceaselessly hostile to men. The Bible teaches that this intelligence is a person, not in the same sense as the Holy Spirit is a person, nor in the same sense as you and I are individual persons; but he has real personality, in some sense comparable to divine and to human personality, but by no means the same as either.

The devil is certainly not a man with horns, hooves and a tail, as he is usually depicted; nor is he a figure to joke and laugh about. Personal pronouns are used to describe him, and we are warned to beware of his subtle wiles. Of course, the devil's best trick is to convince men that he does not exist. If he is non-existent or dead, there must be someone carrying on his devilish work—which was never more evident than it is today. The modern mind may reject the idea of a satanic ruler because of the popular, repulsive and grotesque representation of him the Middle Ages gave the world, but the fact remains that he is gifted with the highest intelligence and is exceedingly powerful. His existence and influence were firmly believed by our Lord and His apostles:

> Then Jesus was led by the Spirit into the desert to be tempted by the devil. After fasting forty days and forty nights, he was hungry. The tempter came to him and said, "If you are the Son of God, tell these stones to become bread." Jesus answered, "It is written: 'Man does not live on bread alone, but on every word that comes from the mouth of God.'" Then the devil took him to the holy city and had him stand on the highest point of the temple. "If you are the Son of God," he said, "throw yourself down. For it is written: 'He

will command his angels concerning you, and they will lift you up in their hands, so that you will not strike your foot against a stone.' " Jesus answered him, "It is written: 'Do not put the Lord your God to the test.' " Again, the devil took him to a very high mountain and showed him all the kingdoms of the world and their splendor. "All this I will give you," he said, "if you will bow down and worship me." Jesus said to him, "Away from me, Satan! For it is written: 'Worship the Lord your God, and serve him only.' " (Matthew 4:1–10; see also Matthew 12:27; Luke 10:17–18; Romans 16:20; 2 Corinthians 11:14, 16; Revelation 12:7–9; 20:2, 10.)

In our study of this subject we consider Satan, his many names, his fall, his fallen angels, his demons and also the victory we gain in Christ.

B. Satan

1. His Many Names

Scripture, the only source of correct information concerning spiritual beings, makes it clear that one of the evil angels is vastly superior to the rest in capacity and influence, possessing far more power than the others, and referred to singly as being the grand enemy of God and man. Satan's name appears fifty-four times in the Bible. Hence Satan is designated by various names and titles of peculiar significance, which apply to one being only, revealing features of his character:

Satan means "the adversary" (1 Peter 5:8, KJV)

Abaddon, Apollyon (Revelation 9:11) both mean "the destroyer"

Lucifer (Isaiah 14:12) means "day-star," "bright one," or "shining one"

Devil (Revelation 12:10) means "accuser," "slanderer"

Dragon (Revelation 12:9) indicates his power

The accuser of our brethren (Revelation 12:10)

The adversary (1 Peter 5:8)

Beelzebub (Matthew 12:24) means "lord of flies" or "prince of demons"

Belial (2 Corinthians 6:15), the low, abject one, means "worthlessness" in Old Testament

The deceiver of the whole world (Revelation 12:9)

An enemy (Matthew 13:28)

The wicked one (Matthew 13:19)

The father of lies (John 8:44)

A murderer from the beginning (John 8:44)

The prince of the power of the air (Ephesians 2:2)

Prince of this world (John 12:31; 14:30; 16:11)

The god of this world (2 Corinthians 4:4)

The prince of demons (Matthew 12:24)

That old serpent (Revelation 12:9)

The tempter (Matthew 4:3; 1 Thessalonians 3:5)

The tormentor (2 Corinthians 12:7)

Surely such an array of dreadful titles reveals the kind of being the devil is and furnishes a reason why we should beware of him! This mighty angel, superior in natural capacity, power and wisdom, excelling all other angels in honour and dignity, and still the principal of the fallen angels, surpasses them in subtlety and cunning. Yet he was not always a devil. Who then is this devil, and how did he become one?

Because the once *bearer of light* became the *prince of darkness,* earning for himself the name *Satan,* adversary of God, of man, of all that is good, is it not folly to underestimate his power or to cultivate an ignorance of his reality? Blindness to the existence of an enemy makes it impossible to conquer him. It is imprudent to underestimate the devil and thereby invite defeat and welcome slavery. If we accept the Scriptures as a divine revelation, then it is incumbent upon us to know something of the devil's original angelic splendour, the intensity of his malice since his fall, and the agony of his future punishment.

While God is the Creator of all angels, strictly speaking He did not create the devil. He created a unique angelic being who, by a free act cutting himself off from God, turned himself into an adversary of God. Originally, the devil was Lucifer, and the highest of the angels, who lost such a name of love by his fall, but who lost nothing of his natural supremacy—which he still exerts over the hierarchy of angels who fell with him.

Lucifer, meaning "light-bearer," is found in Isaiah 14:12–14:

How have you fallen from heaven,
  O morning star, son of the dawn!
You have been cast down to the earth,
  you who once laid low the nations!
You said in your heart, "I will ascend to heaven;
  I will raise my throne above the stars of God;
I will sit enthroned on the mount of assembly,
  on the utmost heights of the sacred mountain.
I will ascend above the tops of the clouds;
  I will make myself like the Most High."

2. The Cause of Satan's Fall

Lucifer became *Satan* at a price. Some writers think that he was then cast out of heaven (Luke 10:18) and then made the air and the earth the scenes of his diabolical activity (Ephesians 2:2; 1 Peter 5:8). The haughty ruler of Babylon and the miserable King of Tyre (Ezekiel 28:12–18) fittingly describe the once glorious chief in heaven. The iniquity by which Lucifer fell was pride, or his being lifted up by reason of his superlative beauty and brightness. "Your heart became proud on account of your beauty, and you corrupted your wisdom because of your splendor. So I threw you to the earth; I made a spectacle of you before kings" (Ezekiel 28:17; see also 1 Timothy 3:6).

He is expressly called an angel (Ezekiel 28:14–16) and a fallen angel. He was the "anointed" cherub, set apart for a divinely-given task. He is spoken of as having dwelt in the garden of God, the paradise of God, the holy mountain of God, the sanctuary (Exodus 38:13; 28:14, 16, 18; Revelation 21:10–21).

Because of the enormous and eternal issues related to Satan's fall, let us examine more fully the causes of his rebellion. That pride and ambition were especially the sins by which Satan fell is sufficiently evident from Paul's warning about being lifted up with pride. Excelling all other angels in power and glory and made something of an equivalent to "Secretary of State" to represent God, Satan was not content with a place of subordination to the will of God: "Now is the time for judgment on this world; now the prince of this world will be driven out" (John 12:31). "I will not speak with you much longer, for the prince of this world is coming. He has no hold on me . . ." (John 14:30). "And in regard to judgment, because the prince of this world now stands condemned" (John 16:11). He rebelled against divine sovereignty and allowed self-will to assert itself in defiance of God's will (Isaiah 14:13, 14; 2 Thessalonians 2:4).

Precisely when Satan rebelled against his Creator is a secret known only to God and Satan. This we do know: there must have arrived in the prehistoric eternity a moment when this world prince of the Most High renounced his allegiance to God, and thereby changed from a "Lucifer," a "light-bearer" of the divine glory, into an "adversary" of God and a "slanderer" of His saints. That he was a fallen celestial being before the world and man were created is evident from the fact that he appeared to Eve as the subtle serpent, and deceived her.

Because of His sovereign will, God gave to angels and men, regardless of the perfection of intellect and will, the ability to choose between good and evil. It was thus that Lucifer used his gift against the Giver. Created in grace and lifted to the supernatural plane, we would have thought that his dazzling quality of angelic perfection would have precluded the very thought of sin.

In what way did Satan fail to make his will one with God's will? The two purely spiritual sins of *pride* and *envy* are possibilities. Since envy demands pride as an absolute prerequisite, it becomes clear that the sin of Lucifer was pride. John Milton, who must be read not as a divine, but as a poet, gave us these dramatic lines in *Paradise Lost*:

Satan; so call him now, his former name
Is heard no more in heaven; he of the first,
If not the first Archangel, great in power,
In favour and pre-eminence, yet fraught

With envy against the Son of God, that day
Honoured by His great Father, and proclaimed
Messiah, King Anointed, could not bear
Through pride, that sight, and thought himself impaired.
He resolved
With all his legions to dislodge, and leave
Unworshipped, unobeyed, the Throne Supreme,
Contemptuous!

The form of pride resulting in the fall of Lucifer was, as Milton suggests, the pride of position. He wanted not only to be equal with or above God (Isaiah 14:12–14), but to thwart the divine purpose for the Son of God and for the sons of men. To quote the Roman Catholic writer, Walter Farrell:

Lucifer might have been envious of the future exaltation of human nature by its union to the Son of God in His Incarnation; of the future exaltation of men to angelic, nay to divine heights by sanctifying grace and the promise of heaven . . . . Some considered Satan's sin as properly one of pride, but would have it consist in a disordered desire for a hypostatic (essential) union between the Word of God and his own angelic nature.

Some of the writers argue that the devil rebelled against God because of His desire to make men like angels and to take the place of fallen angels. The redemptive purpose of God, however, is not to give men the vacated thrones of evil angels but to fashion all who believe into His church. Jonathan Edwards (1703–1758), the penetrating theologian, advanced the view:

. . . that the angels, learning of the setting up of a kingdom for the man Christ Jesus, and of the divine purpose that the human nature was to be united to the Second Person of the Trinity, and that He was to be the Head of all principality and power, became envious of their own position.

God having thus declared His great love for mankind, Satan, or Lucifer, being the archangel, the very highest and brightest of all

God's creatures, could not bear it, thought it below him and a great debasing of his exalted position. So he conceived rebellion against the Almighty, and drew a vast company with him: their refusing to be subject to Christ, as man thus assumed, was their first sin and in opposition set up another kingdom against Him.

It was thus through pride that Lucifer became Satan, the "black sheep" in the family of God, His Judas. Through this opposition to God he brought a curse upon himself. God never cursed sinful man, but the serpent is under a curse that can never be repealed. Man's pride makes him a friend of the Devil. How true it is that the Devil sleeps like a dangerous animal in the shadow of good works, whence we conceive a secret admiration for ourselves. Wise are those who foil him by making themselves poor in spirit.

A fact that we must not lose sight of is that the devil, although a fallen angelic being, is still an angel. True, he is a rebel angel, but he is still an angel created by God with and among the other celestial spirits; even his fall and disgrace did not deprive him of the angelic nature. Satan retains the privileges of his unchanged nature and is still able to display his original grandeur (2 Corinthians 11:14). Although now the angel of darkness, the devil persists because, in spite of everything, he is still an angel. We do not know the breathless height of perfection from which Satan fell: we only know that he carried such perfection with him into darkness.

By his angelic nature, the devil enjoys that independence distinctively characteristic of a pure spirit. Because of his angelic independence he is immune to pain, to injury, to sickness, to death; indeed, he is even immune to human discomfort. There are in him, then, no parts to be dismembered, no possibilities of corruption and decay, no threat of a separation of parts that will result in death. He is incorruptible, immune to the vagaries, the pains, the limitations of the flesh, immortal. Only God, by His almighty power, could destroy Satan, recalling the borrowed existence by which the devil lives; and this God will not do. Angels are spirits as opposed to flesh and blood. "For our struggle is not against flesh and blood, but against the rulers, against the authorities, against the powers of this dark world and against the spiritual forces of evil in the heavenly realms" (Ephesians 6:12; also Luke 24:39).

One of the most startling characteristics of the devil, to us who savour drops of time so thirstily, is his agelessness. Says Walter Farrell:

> It staggers us to see him as young now as when the world was born, with all the undiminished energy and dynamic vigour of full, young maturity. Yet the fact is plain enough: a spirit does not grow up any more than it grows down; there is no way in which an angel can age, no moment in which it does not possess the full strength of its angelic life. From the very first instant of his existence down through the whole length of eternity the Devil lacks nothing of his angelic perfection. He has watched the world grow old and the generations of men and women pass in unending procession from birth to death; when the last of that long line has passed, and the sun has set for the last time, Satan will still be young.

But, although created to prominence in the realm of angels and of men, Satan is doomed to eternal remorse and torment. Cast out of heaven (Luke 10:18), then to the earth (Revelation 12:9), he is to be fettered for 1,000 years in the bottomless pit (Revelation 20:1–3) before being thrown into the lake of fire, the final depository of the devil, his fallen angels, and the wicked. "And the devil, who deceived them, was thrown into the lake of burning sulfur, where the beast and the false prophet had been thrown. They will be tormented day and night for ever and ever" (Revelation 20:10).

Engulfed by the blackest despair, and bitterly hating himself for his plight and for his burning opposition to God, Satan's terrible doom has been announced. Shakespeare gave us the lines:

> When he falls, he falls like Lucifer,
> Never to hope again.

To Augustine two spiritual powers have contested for the allegiance of God's creation ever since the fall of the angels: faith and unbelief. "Good and bad angels have arisen . . . not from a difference in their *origin* and *nature* but from a difference in their *wills* and *desires*. . . . Some steadfastly continued in that which was the common good for all, namely in God himself, and in His eternity, truth and love; . . . others became proud, deceived, envious."

C. Fallen Angels

1. Those Who Are Free

And there was war in heaven. Michael and his angels fought against the dragon, and the dragon and his angels fought back. But he was not strong enough, and they lost their place in heaven. The great dragon was hurled down—that ancient serpent called the devil, or Satan, who leads the whole world astray. He was hurled to the earth, and his angels with him. (Revelation 12:7–9)

When we say "free," we do not mean they are free from sin or final judgment. They are still of their father, the devil. However, for the time being they are free to roam this world and to deceive. Peter said of the devil, "Your enemy the devil prowls around like a roaring lion looking for someone to devour" (1 Peter 5:8). So the devil and his cohorts are under condemnation, but until their day of judgment they are free to deceive and possess those who respond to their temptation.

The apostasy of angels is clearly taught in different parts of Scripture. A vast number of intelligent beings, how many we have no way of knowing, lost their pristine honour and happiness, their primeval virtue and dignity. Excelling all others in knowledge, power and splendour, they rose up in rebellion against the Creator, Benefactor, and Sovereign and sunk to the depths of sin, shame and misery, earning for themselves thereby endless hatred and contempt. Like the devil, their leader, they too were drowned in conceit. Through pride they fell, and since their fall they have laboured to effect universal rebellion against the laws of God. Dreadful punishment awaits these angels transformed into evil, malignant spirits and demons. When they sinned against God, divine thunder dashed them into hell, and for them there is the blackness of darkness for ever and ever.

When man fell, however, God provided a remedy for his sin; through His mercy He delivers the fallen creature from misery. Man tumbles down, and divine goodness holds out a hand to lift him up

(Hebrews 3:14). We were as fit objects of justice as angels, and angels as fit objects of goodness as we; they were prime and golden pieces of creation, not laden with human nature, yet they lie under the ruins of their fall, while man has the opportunity through grace and acceptance to be refined for another world.

> From heaven the sinning angels fell,
> And wrath and darkness chained them down:
> But man, vile man, forsook his bliss,
> And mercy lifts him to a crown!
>
> Amazing work of sovereign grace,
> That could distinguish rebels so!
> Our guilty treasons called aloud
> For everlasting fetters too!
>
> To Thee, to Thee, Almighty Love!
> Our souls, ourselves, our all we pay!
> Millions of tongues shall sound Thy praise,
> On the bright hills of heavenly day!
> (Author unknown)

From Scripture we learn that some fallen angels are free to roam the earth. Others, we read, are not free but bound.

2. Those Who Are Bound

For if God did not spare angels when they sinned, but sent them to hell, putting them into gloomy dungeons to be held for judgment... (2 Peter 2:4)

These angels are not to be confused with those who are free to roam and act at the bidding of their satanic lord. Originally they were one with the rebellious host; but somewhere, somehow, these angels, presently in captivity, became separated from the rest and were thrust by God into darkness. These are the fallen angels who left their first estate and are reserved unto the final judgment. Their revolt must have been more deeply and more heinously criminal, to have deserved the immediate loss of their freedom and millennia of severe bondage. The liberty they had after their expulsion from heaven was taken from them.

There are two specific references to the present plight of these chained and doomed angels. Jude writes, "And the angels who did not keep their positions of authority but abandoned their own home—these he has kept in darkness, bound with everlasting chains for judgment on the great Day" (Jude 6). Also Peter writes, " . . . God did not spare angels when they sinned, but sent them to hell, putting them into gloomy dungeons to be held for judgment . . ." (2 Peter 2:4). The casual reader can see that these two verses refer to the same class of sinning angels. It may help us to determine the occasion of the severance of this section of the angelic host from the rest of the fallen company if we examine the language and context of each passage.

The language about angels that "sinned," e.g., "the angels for their sin" (2 Peter 2:4), points to some definite sin. What particular sin is implied? Not that which preceded the history of the human race, commonly known as the fall of angels, of which there is no record in the Old Testament. That they fell is evident, but when they fell is not revealed. These angels, who were not spared punishment, were cast down to hell. The word translated hell is "tartarus," the deepest pit of gloom. Although such a terrible abyss of darkness must be awful, it is only a temporary abode. A still more dreadful prison awaits these evil angels.

Jude is somewhat more explicit and reminds us that these angels were so punished because they left their first estate, failed to keep their own dignity, forsook their own principality. They lost not only their freedom but their power or rule through entrance into a forbidden realm of bondage; these angels have ceased to trouble the human race. Of them Adam Clarke writes:

St. Jude says, "they kept not their first estate, but fell from their own "habitation"; which seems to indicate that they got disconnected with their lot, and aspired to higher honours, or perhaps to celestial domination. The tradition of their fall is in all countries and in all religions, but the accounts given are various and contradictory; no wonder, for we have no direct revelation on the subject.

D. The Power of Demons

Demons were originally among the faithful angels, but fell with Satan, although just when or why they fell has not been fully revealed. We can only surmise that they fell into condemnation through pride.

Belief in the existence and power of evil spirits has prevailed among all the known peoples of the world from earliest times. However, the conception of demonic activity and possession as found among the Babylonians or Assyrians or in Jewish apocryphal literature is not our present concern. Because Jesus came as "the truth," what He taught is, for us, the authoritative word. We reject the idea that He accommodated Himself to the teaching prevalent among the Jews concerning the reality and operations of evil spirits. Never for a moment did Jesus doubt the presence and power of demons. Coming to earth as the Son of God, He was familiar with the fall of Lucifer and his angels. He was present in the dateless past when this rebellion took place. Thus the Gospels portray Christ as "the great exorcist," whose very presence terrified the demons, and at whose command, as we shall see, they were compelled to leave their tortured victims.

Our Lord, in His struggles against Satan and his hosts, "*cast out demons*" (Mark 1:39), and cured those who were "*troubled by unclean spirits,*" (Luke 6:18) and "*the demon-possessed*" (Matthew 4:24). When the emissaries of John the Baptist came to ask Jesus whether He was really the Messiah, He noted that He cured many who had diseases and hurts and evil spirits (Luke 7:21). The evil spirits themselves, we also note, asked if He was the Messiah. Out of Mary Magdalene He cast "seven demons" (Luke 8:2; Mark 16:9). Then He commissioned His disciples to "*drive out demons,*" to have "*authority over evil spirits,*" and never to disparage the expulsion of evil spirits (Matthew 10:8; Mark 6:7; 9:38; Luke 9:1–49). Returning from their mission, the disciples rejoiced because the demons had been subject unto them in Christ's name (Luke 10:17–20). Herod's threats were met with the challenge, "*I drive out demons*" (Luke 13:32). Following His death and ascension, the power thus exercised by Jesus became the prerogative of His disciples (Mark 16:17, 18; Acts 8:7; 16:16–18; 19:12–17).

The Gospels, then, are eloquent concerning the fact that Christ believed in the reality of demons, and, more importantly, concerning His supremacy over them. The Almighty has locked and bolted our human nature against the intrusion of the demon-world, and it is at our peril that we open the door from within or allow it to be broken in from without. The angels will not attempt to help us unless at the express command of the Almighty; but demon-spirits are disobedient and stubborn. Demons operate above the laws of the natural realm. They are invisible and without material substance.

1. Demons are spirits (Matthew 12:43, 45).

2. Demons are numerous . . . so numerous that Mark 5:9 describes one demon as saying, "My name is Legion, for we are many."

3. Demons can control men (Mark 5:2–5).

4. Demons are unclean and violent (Matthew 8:28–31).

5. Demons know Jesus Christ as the Most High God. They recognize His supreme authority (Mark 1:23, 24; Acts 19:15; James 2:19).

6. They are aware of their eternal fate. "*What do you want with us, Son of God?*" they shouted. "*Have you come here to torture us before the appointed time?*" (Matthew 8:29).

7. Demons are in conflict with Christians (Ephesians 6:12). "*The Spirit clearly says that in later times some will abandon the faith and follow deceiving spirits and things taught by demons*" (1 Timothy 4:1).

8. Unbelievers are susceptible to demon possession. "*As for you [believers], you were dead in your transgressions and sins, in which you used to live when you followed the ways of this world and of the ruler of the kingdom of the air, the spirit who is now at work in those who are disobedient*" (Ephesians 2:1, 2).

Demons are a type of fallen angelic being possessing terrible strength, by which they invade the human body with such disabilities as blindness (Matthew 12:22), insanity (Luke 8:26–36), muteness (Matthew 9:32–33), and suicidal mania (Mark 9:22). (However, it must be remembered that not every physical nor mental affliction is a result of demonism.) That Christ actually spoke to demons and heard their replies shows that they are real beings, and not merely ancient personifications of illnesses (Matthew 8:28–34).

E. Christ, the Way to Victory

You, dear children, are from God and have overcome them, because the one who is in you is greater than the one who is in the world. (1 John 4:4)

In many ways the first Epistle of John is one of the most remarkable letters in the New Testament. It is a precious pearl of divine revelation, particularly in connection with Satan and his nature and works. It is a family letter from the father to his dear children who are in the world surrounded by evil forces. John writes, "*My dear children, I write this to you so that you will not sin. But if anybody does sin, we have one who speaks to the Father in our defense—Jesus Christ, the Righteous One*" (1 John 2:1).

The epistle is full of sharp contrasts, which even a casual reading makes clear: Christ and antichrist; God and the devil; light and darkness; life and death; holiness and sin; love and hate; the truthful and the liars; the overcomers and the defeated; the Savior, who is the leader of the good, and Satan, who is the monarch of all who are evil. The epistle is, therefore, a gallery of battles and represents the greatest of all conflicts in history, namely, the war between *good* and *evil*. The comforting and inspiring message for the heart of God's children is that "*the one who is in you is greater than the one who is in the world*"—"*the one who is in you*" referring to our all-conquering God; "*the one who is in the world*" meaning Satan, the antagonist of God and man (1 John 4:4).

The Bible never attempts to dispute or deny the greatness of Satan's wisdom and might. He was created the highest of all angelic beings when "*all the angels [of God] shouted for joy*" (Job 38:7). As an archangel he possessed a marvelous intellect, along with unique and perfect knowledge, but through pride his original greatness was perverted, and since his fall, his power has been used to blast rather than bless. His great hold on humanity may be attributed to the fact that he has assailed every soul since Eve. Satan preferred, as John Milton puts it, rather to

> Reign in Hell than serve in Heaven
> And with ambitious aim
> Against the Throne and Monarchy of God,
> Raised impious war in Heaven.

But although he continues his impious war, aided by his legions of darkness, the devil is a defeated foe. One greater than he appeared and by his life, death and resurrection robbed him of his power and authority and destroyed his works. Fight on he may, but he knows only too well that One greater than he is in the world to liberate those in his cruel bondage.

> What though in the conflict for right
> Your enemies almost prevail!
> God's armies just hid from sight
> Are more than the foes which assail.
> (Author Unknown)

How the saints John wrote to must have been heartened by his inspired declarations regarding the conquest of Satan by Christ! They lived in days permeated with the spirit of antichrist, and overcame the influence of false teachers by the faith that Jesus indwelling them was far greater than the god of this world. Being begotten of God, they were protected from seduction by the wicked one (1 John 5:18). The supreme purpose of the Incarnation was the destruction of the works of the devil (1 John 3:8). This superior greatness of Jesus is based upon the fact that although Satan has power, he is not *all powerful* like the risen Christ, who is omnipotent, omniscient, and omnipresent and is also the sinless Lord.

Satan may possess potent forces united in their diabolical purpose (for Satan never casts out Satan), but he does not share the omnipotence of deity. Christ met His adversary alone, and single-handedly assailed the host of wickedness, and triumphed gloriously over them. Had He wished, He could have summoned a host of faithful angels to assist, but like David of old, He preferred to meet His Goliath alone, and thereby make his disaster and defeat more overwhelming. The strong man has been bound by the One who has the preeminence and is Lord of all.

Christ is not only all-powerful but also all-wise, all-knowing, all-intelligent. Great wisdom was certainly bestowed upon Satan when he was created as Lucifer, but he was not given omniscience, which is the prerogative of deity alone. He can understand the subtleties of the human heart and reach it by choosing from a thousand forms of temptation he has developed through many millennia. But Christ is far wiser, in that He can discern satanic approaches afar off. He can read the devil's mind, but the devil cannot read His mind. This is clear from our Lord's warning to Peter, "Simon, Simon, Satan has asked to sift you as wheat." Able, then, to discern his evil intentions, Christ is likewise able to circumvent them.

Omnipresence is another quality deity alone possesses; man can never flee from God's presence, even if he goes to the uttermost parts of the sea (Psalm 139). As the result of His resurrection and the advent of the Holy Spirit, Jesus promised His own that He would be with them always, no matter where they were in the world (Matthew 28:20). But Satan cannot be everywhere at the same time, as his conqueror can. We concede that he has universal influence, for the whole world is in the lap of such a wicked one, but his actual presence, like his power, is limited. It is common for us to say that certain persons are doing certain things when actually their agents are acting on their behalf and in their name and authority. A commanding general cannot be on every part of the battlefield at the same time, but his officers execute his orders and carry out his commands. Likewise, an ambassador represents the head of his country, and speaks and acts on his behalf.

This is so with Satan, who is not able to work in all hearts at the same time. Yet, through all the evil subordinates under his control and mastery, he can fulfill his base designs. Thoroughly imbued with his spirit, roaming hordes of demons act as he would. He is in contact with all "his angels," having a sort of sense by which he can communicate orders and receive reports. How we bless the Lord for His omnipresence, enabling Him to promise that no matter where we may go in the world, He will never leave nor forsake us!

The testimony of John in his matchless epistle is that Jesus is the personification of unblemished holiness. He is light and in Him is no darkness at all. But Satan is likened to the darkness. Darkness is the absence of light—a negation. Light is not the absence of darkness only, but something real and positive.

Christ is portrayed as infinite holiness, and, as the light of the world, He can positively banish all darkness. Because of His perfection, He can dispel all evil and satanic influences and ultimately will disperse them, for in glory there is "no night there."

Likewise, in his Christ-glorifying gospel, John assures us of his Master's holiness and consequent victory over the evil one. His is the gospel of triumph! The apostle records that Jesus used the designation of Satan, "the prince of this world," twice, but with a different association in each case. First, Jesus assured His disciples that *"Now is the judgment of this world: now shall the prince of this world be cast out"* (John 12:31, KJV). Weymouth translates it, *"Now comes judgment upon this world: now will the Prince of this world be driven out!"*

The Greek word for "judgment" used here means *crisis,* and refers to something to be accomplished by the death of Jesus. The judgment of all mankind is still in the future. Anticipating his death by crucifixion, Jesus declares a victory over Satan's domain with divine exultation and triumph. Calvary was to mean the emancipation of souls from satanic bondage—the *crisis,* when provision would be secured from sin's defilement and dominion. As Barnes expresses it in his monumental *Notes on the New Testament:*

Now is approaching the decisive scene, the eventful period—the crisis—when it shall be determined who shall rule the world. There has been a long conflict between the powers of light and darkness—between God and the Devil. Satan has so far effectually ruled, that he may be said to be the prince of this world. "But my approaching death will be the means of setting up the kingdom of God over man." The death of Christ was to be the most grand and effectual of all means that could be used to establish the authority of the law and the government of God, Rom 8:3,4 . . . The death of Jesus was the determining cause, the grand crisis, the concentration of all that God had ever done, or will ever do, to break down the kingdom of Satan, and set up His power over man . . . It was the fulfillment of the prediction of Genesis 3:15. ("And I will put enmity between you and the woman, and between your offspring and hers; he will crush your head, and you will strike his heel.")

Jesus was born holy and undefiled. The angel said to the Virgin Mary, "*The Holy Spirit will come upon you, and the power of the Most High will overshadow you. So the holy one to be born will be called the Son of God*" (Luke 1:35). This is why He is separate from sinners, all of whom were conceived in sin and "*shapen in iniquity*" (Psalm 51:5, KJV), meaning that because of original sin they were born with evil propensities.

Jesus, however, was born with an unsinning nature, and thus appealed to the knowledge His accusers had of His sinless life: "*Can any of you prove me guilty of sin?*" (John 8:46). He also reminded them of His entire conformity to His Father's will: ". . . I always do what pleases him [my Father]" (John 8:29). He was thus distinct from all others, for never had He cast a shadow on the brightness of the vision of His father's presence by the least sympathy with evil. Through all his thirty-three years Jesus remained as pure as God in heaven, passing through a world of sin and satanic allurements as a sunbeam passing through a hovel without a shadow. There was no territory in His being to which Satan could lay claim, nothing in Him that had affinity with sin. When he said to His disciples, "the prince of this world is coming," the reference was to the effort of Satan to try Him in the dreadful conflict of the temptation in Gethsemane and Calvary. But He faced the powers of darkness as the thrice Holy One, and triumphed gloriously over them.

Sinners are born with one nature; namely, one prone to evil. Jesus was born with one nature; namely, an unsinning one. The saints have two natures, namely, the old Adamic nature and the new nature in Christ Jesus. The character of, and conflict between, these dual natures is fully dealt with by Paul in Romans 7 and 8. ". . . When I would do good, evil is present with me" (Romans 7:21, KJV). The conflict of the Holy Spirit with the flesh, the enmity between the spirit and the carnal mind, are constant in the experience of the true child of God. But greater is He who is in us than he who is in the world, and through His finished work of the cross we can live in triumph (2 Corinthians 2:14).

> The gates of brass before Him burst,
> The iron fetters yield.

We are doomed to failure if we try to meet Satan on his own ground. Our only hope of victory is to meet him in the virtue and power of the Redeemer. There is a story of a swan wobbling along the shore of a lake, when a hungry wolf appeared and would have torn the swan to pieces. But the swan said to itself, "If I am not strong on land, I am strong in the water." So in it plunged and the wolf followed. The swan turned around and with its strong bill gripped the ear of the wolf and dragged its head under the water and held it there until the beast was drowned. If we assail the satanic wolf in our own strength and on its ground, we are bound to lose in the conflict. It is only as we meet the wolf on the Lord's ground that we experience what it is to be more than conquerors (Revelation 12:10, 11).

A friend once asked an aged saint what caused him so often to complain of pain and weariness at eventide. "Alas!" he replied, "I have every day so much to do. I have two falcons to tame, two hares to keep from running away, two hawks to manage, a serpent to confine, a lion to chain, and a sick man to tend and wait upon." The friend said to the old man, "You must be joking. Surely no man can have all these things to do at once?" He replied, "Indeed, I am not joking. What I told you is the sad, sober truth; for the two falcons are my two eyes, which I must diligently guard; the two hares are my feet, which want to run in the way of sin; the two hawks are my two hands which I must train to work and provide for myself and my brethren in need; the serpent is my tongue I must bridle lest I speak unnecessarily; the lion is my heart with which I continually fight lest evil things come out of it; the sick man is my whole body always needing watchfulness and care. All this wears out my daily strength!"

Our obligation is to be aware of the devil's present evil design of causing misery and sin and to avail ourselves of the victory over the devil. Calvary was his Waterloo, and faith overcomes the accuser of the brethren by the blood of the Lamb. Ignatius in *Discernment of Spirits* says: "Unmask Satan and you vanquish him." James reminds us: "*Submit yourselves, then, to God. Resist the devil, and he will flee from you*" (James 4:7). The only effective weapon to defeat him is the infallible Word of God (Matthew 4:4; Ephesians 6:17; Matthew 12:28).

Our responsibility is threefold: We are to watch against Satan (1 Peter 5:8), to give no place to him (Ephesians 4:27), and to resist him (James 4:7). Our enemy is free on earth to the length of his chain, but no further (Job 2:5). He cannot go beyond God's permission nor injure God's elect. His freedom of range in the air and on earth is that of a chained prisoner under sentence. By faith we must appropriate the victory over all satanic powers Christ secured by His death and resurrection.

> A good example is the driving out of the evil spirits from the Gerasene demoniac. Here we find a radical demonstration of the power of God to dispel evil from our lives (Mark 5:1–20). In setting this tormented man free from the demonic spirits which were in possession of his mind, Jesus gave clear evidence of his ability to overcome Satan's grip on us. This miraculous victory over the agents of Satan gives support to the Apostle John's bold contention that, "The reason the Son of God appeared was to destroy the works of the devil" (1 John 3:8). (From a sermon by John H. Stevens.)

We have the blessed promise that the Lord is able and willing to deliver us from every evil work and preserve us unto His heavenly kingdom (2 Timothy 4:18). Let us claim the strength of our omnipotent Lord and rest in Him, confident that He will vanquish the foe seeking to ensnare us. Before long we shall be saved to sin no more.

Dr. Robert M. M'Cheyne would have us sing:

When I stand before the throne
Dressed in beauty not my own,
When I see Thee as Thou art,

Love Thee with unsinning heart;
Then, Lord, shall I full know—
Not till then—how much I owe.

If there has been any tampering with the demon-world, the ur-
gency for immediate arrest is imperative, lest the current become too
swift to be arrested by the oarsman, though he pull against it with the
agony of despair.

Angels, your march oppose
Who still in strength excel,
Creatures, invisible:
With rage that never ends,
Their hellish arts they try;
Legions of dire, malicious fiends,
And spirits enthroned on high.

Go up with Christ your Head;
Your Captain's footsteps see;
Follow your Captain, and be led
To certain victory.
All power to him is given;
He ever reigns the same.
Salvation, happiness and heaven
Are all in Jesus' name.

Only have faith in God;
In faith your foes assail;
Not wrestling against flesh and blood,
But all the power of hell
From thrones of glory driven,
By flamey vengeance hurl'd,
They throng the air, and darken heaven,
And rule the lower world. (John Wesley)

SECTION TWO

■ ■ ■

The Ministry of Angels

6

Angels in the Old Testament

For he will command his angels concerning you to guard you in all your ways; they will lift you up in their hands, so that you will not strike your foot against a stone. (Psalm 91:11–12)

A. Introduction

From first to last, the angels of God are ministering spirits. Worship and ministry are their twofold function—they are priests in the heavenly temple; messengers on God's errands of love and justice (Isaiah 6:1–3; Daniel 7:9–10). Angelic activity covers all history, ancient and modern, national and personal. The world is in closer touch with heavenly forces than it dreams.

In this dim world of clouding cares,
We rarely know, till 'wildered eyes
See white wings lessening up the skies,
The angels with us unawares. (Author Unknown)

From the earliest ages angels have been employed to make known the decrees and purposes of God concerning His dispensations of mercy to mankind. But what methods they themselves employ in their ministry we are not told, lest we worship them instead of the Master directing their ministrations.

The Biblical understanding of the mission and ministry of angels imparts a sense of the greatness of heaven's resources and a view of divine goodness for which we should be grateful. The chief end of the service of angels is the glory of God and the good of humankind. Angels, at God's command, have succoured His servants in prosecuting the high commissions of their Redeemer; and these exalted celestial beings will continue to minister unto them in His name, until "*the kingdoms of this world [shall have] become the kingdoms of our Lord, and of His Christ*" (Revelation 11:15, KJV).

It is to be feared that the presence and power of angels are not as real to us as they should be. While we have no way of knowing how often our feet are directed into right paths, or how often we are guarded from harm, seen or unseen, or how subject we are to angelic suggestion, our invisible companions are ever at hand. They form our protective shield, and over and above them is the everlasting God and Father they serve and we love. So why should we charge our souls with care?

The appearances of the angels of God to men in ancient times are frequently mentioned in the Scriptures. This record of the invisible and visible manifestation of these divine messengers reveals how large a part they perform in the economy of God.

God created the angels for a specific purpose. What they do in His immediate presence, apart from worshipping and adoring Him, we are not told. Angelic appearances among men reveal the service of the faithful angels as one of encouragement and care. Angels carry out God's will on behalf of men and assist His children in their pilgrim walk. At the close of his colourful life Jacob could say, "*The angel which redeemed me from all evil . . .*" (Genesis 48:16, KJV). Bible saints, and God's people of all ages, have testified to the solicitude and protection of the angels. Briefly, then, let us think of those Bible characters of the Old Testament favoured with visitations of these celestial beings who journey to men on God's behalf.

B. Adam and Eve: Kept out of Eden by an Angel

After he drove the man out, he placed on the east side of the Garden of Eden cherubim and a flaming sword flashing back and forth to guard the way to the tree of life. (Genesis 3:24)

Probably no one ever read with a devout and serious mind the inspiring story relating to our first parents—their creation, their first habitation in Eden, their fall from holiness and happiness by transgression, and their expulsion from the blessed abode of Paradise—without feeling a desire to know more concerning those surpassingly interesting events. Happy for us, however, that we have so large a measure of satisfying information; and "what we know not now, we shall know hereafter," perhaps from the lips of Adam and Eve, in the heavenly paradise of God.

The cherubim and the flaming sword placed to guard the way to the tree of life have been the subjects of much anxious and learned inquiry. Great obscurity still remains in relation to them; partly, at least, because of the brevity of the account concerning them in the sacred history. Some have considered the account given by Moses as a kind of allegory or metaphorical representation of the banishment of man from paradise. "Cherubim," however, as is generally agreed, denote a class of celestial living creatures—a kind of angelic beings, spirits of a superior order, immediate attendants on the throne of God, ready to execute his high commissions.

"Cherubim" were thus stationed at the entrance of the garden of God—in an honourable office—for the benefit of Adam and Eve, even though on account of their disobedience they were expelled from the delightful seats of paradise. Milton, therefore, in his lofty strains, represents the divine commission for the performance of this high service in these terms:

> Michael, this my behest have thou in charge;
> Take to thee from among the *Cherubim*
> Thy choice of flaming warriors, lest the fiend,
> Or in behalf of man, or to invade
> Vacant possession, some new trouble raise:
> Haste thee, and from the Praise of God,
> Without remorse drive out the sinful pair,
> From hallowed ground, th' unholy—
> To send them forth, though sorrowing yet in peace:
> And on the east side of the garden place,
> Where entrance up from Eden easiest climbs,

Cherubic watch, and of a sword the flame,
Wide waving; all approach far off to fright,
And guard all passage to the tree of life. (*Paradise Lost*, Book 11)

Paradise, as planted specially by the hand of God for the first human pair in innocence and richly furnished by his overflowing benevolence, was no longer a suitable place of habitation for fallen creatures. Their offended Sovereign designed that they should feel their helpless misery as the fruit of their transgression. By their criminal violation of the easy law of God, they had forfeited every expression of favour from their bountiful Creator. But the mercy of God, by the Mediator, preserved them from despair. Still, though "grace reigned through righteousness, unto eternal life by Jesus Christ our Lord," made known unto them in the promise and by sacrifices, they must suffer the loss of much of their enjoyment and depart from the lovely garden of Eden. The continued sight of the "tree of knowledge of good and evil" might serve to aggravate their wretchedness; and, constantly beholding the "tree of life," they might be tempted to abandon faith in the promised Saviour, to cherish a groundless presumption and endeavour to secure immortality by improper means, not ordained or approved by the gracious God.

God cut off from them all hopes of re-entering the blissful boundaries of paradise in Eden: but it is not said that the cherubim were placed to keep them and their posterity forever from the tree of life. Eternal praises be to God, there is a higher, celestial garden, and a tree of immortal life to which even the Lord directed Adam to look by believing on the promised seed! Our first parents, therefore, lived by faith in the word of the Lord, as all Christians have done; and to our delighted eyes, the New Testament discloses angels ministering without a flaming sword to those who are heirs of salvation, while our blessed Lord and Saviour invites us to rejoice in the words of grace and peace: "*To him who overcomes, I will give the right to eat from the tree of life, which is in the paradise of God*" (Revelation 2:7).

They looking back, all th' eastern side beheld
Of Paradise, so late their happy seat,
Wav'd over by that flaming brand, the gate
With dreadful faces throng'd and fiery arms:

Some natural tears they dropt, but wip'd them soon.
The world was all before them, where to choose
Their place of rest, and Providence their guide:
They hand in hand, with wand'ring steps and slow,
Through Eden took their solitary way. (*Paradise Lost*, Book 12)

C. Abraham: Entertained and Restrained by the Angels

Do not forget to entertain strangers, for by so doing some people
have entertained angels without knowing it. (Hebrews 13:2)

Sitting at his tent door in the plains of Mamre, Abraham revealed
the amiableness of hospitality. Jewish writers identified "the three
men" Abraham entertained as three angels, and gave their names as
Michael, Gabriel and Raphael. Several of the early Christian Fathers,
however, identified them as visible representatives of the adorable
Trinity, which is somewhat fanciful. That they were angelic beings is
plain from the narrative; and from the testimony of Moses, one
possessed more than created excellence and some sign of superiority.

At first, Abraham did not understand the quality of his guests, nor
imagine them as celestial messengers bringing to him joyful tidings
from the Lord of the birth of Isaac, the son of promise. Abraham's last
and greatest trial came when he was commanded to offer up his
beloved son, Isaac, for a burnt offering. He raised the knife to thrust
it into his son's heart...

But the angel of the Lord called out to him from heaven, "Abraham! Abraham!" "Here I am," he replied. "Do not lay a hand on
the boy," he said. "Do not do anything to him. Now I know that
you fear God, because you have not withheld from me your son,
your only son." Abraham looked up and there in a thicket he saw
a ram caught by its horns. He went over and took the ram and
sacrificed it as a burnt offering instead of his son. So Abraham
called that place The Lord Will Provide. And to this day it is said,
"On the mountain of the Lord it will be provided." The angel of
the Lord called to Abraham from heaven a second time and said,
"I swear by myself, declares the Lord, that because you have done

this and have not withheld your son, your only son, I will surely bless you and make your descendants as numerous as the stars in the sky and as the sand on the seashore. Your descendants will take possession of the cities of their enemies, and through your off-spring all nations on earth will be blessed, because you have obeyed me." (Genesis 22:11–18)

D. Hagar: Consoled by an Angel

God heard the boy crying, and the angel of God called to Hagar from heaven and said to her, "What is the matter, Hagar? Do not be afraid; God has heard the boy crying as he lies there. Lift the boy up and take him by the hand, for I will make him into a great nation." (Genesis 21:17–18)

How solicitous the holy angels are! Divine benevolence mercifully interposed for Hagar and Ishmael, her son by Abraham, whose name and birth the angel of the Lord foretold (Genesis 16:7–12; 21:14). Everything was wrong here. There was a shameful distrust of God. Abraham should have believed the promise of God as to his posterity and not complied with Sarah's suggestion in taking Hagar as wife. As the result of the birth of Ishmael, son of the bond-woman, animosity between Ishmael and Isaac, and through them the Arab and the Jew, has persisted through the centuries (Galatians 4:23–31).

Out in the wilderness with her unborn child, Hagar, fatigued and sorrowful, sat down to rest and to refresh herself at the fountain. But her plight, cries and tears were observed by the angel, who called her and said: *"Hagar, servant of Sarai, where have you come from, and where are you going?"* (Genesis 16:8). This heavenly messenger revealed his perfect knowledge of her name and straits and was ready to succour this helpless afflicted woman. Convinced of the authority of her celestial visitant, Hagar returned to her mistress and Ishmael was born.

When Isaac was born, Ishmael looked upon him with jealousy and growing envy, an attitude Hagar doubtless encouraged. Sarah, provoked, insisted that Hagar and Ishmael be expelled from the household. Away from the household, mother and son presented a pitiable sight. Hagar, in her despondency, had forgotten the promise made to her by the angel. Her past assurance, "You are the God who sees me" (Genesis 16:13), was not her present stay. But again the angelic voice was heard, "*What is the matter, Hagar?*" and seasonable relief was afforded to mother and son.

> As Hagar wandered with her child,
> Amid Beersheba's desert wild,
> Their cruse of water failed at last—
> Where no refreshing streamlet passed,
> And 'neath a shrubby arbour nigh,
> Young Ishmael laid him down to die.
>
> But, hark! the Angel of the Lord,
> Lone Hagar's drooping heart restored.
> "Go, raise," he cried, "the fainting boy,
> For he shall prove a mother's joy,
> And mighty nations yet shall be
> Descendants of thy son and thee." (Dr. Knox)

E. Eliezer: Guided by an Angel

> The Lord, the God of heaven, who brought me out of my father's household and my native land and who spoke to me and promised me on oath, saying, 'To your offspring I will give this land'—he will send his angel before you so that you can get a wife for my son from there. (Genesis 24:7)

This charming account of the search for a wife for Isaac is "a love lyric full of romance and tender beauty." But, as Henry Thorne in his exposition of Genesis reminds us:

> In looking for Rebekah, Abraham was really looking for Jesus. Her marriage with Isaac was to be a link in the chain of events which would lead up to "That far-off Divine event For which the whole creation moves."

The mission of Abraham's servant was to find a wife for his master's son, and in his search he had the companionship and guidance of God's angel. Thus heaven and earth united in the choice of Isaac's partner for life. There seems little doubt that the exalted angel, whose guidance Abraham relied on, was the *Angel of the Divine Presence* (Isaiah 63:9), the *Angel of the Covenant* (Malachi 3:1), the *Lord Jesus* Himself.

F. Lot: Delivered by the Angels

> With the coming of dawn, the angels urged Lot, saying, "Hurry! Take your wife and your two daughters who are here, or you will be swept away when the city is punished." When he hesitated, the men grasped his hand and the hands of his wife and of his two daughters and led them safely out of the city, for the Lord was merciful to them. (Genesis 19:15–16)

Lot's residence among the guilty Sodomites affords another illustration of the effectiveness of angelic ministry. The deliverance of Abraham's nephew from destruction by the two angels declares the love of angels for men.

When Lot became aware of the atrocious designs of the sinful Sodomites to abuse his guests, he also discovered their celestial character and found he had been entertaining angels unawares. Angelic kindness surrounded Lot until he was safe out of Sodom, the dreadful overthrow of which was a just judgment upon a guilty people.

The angels God sent to Sodom may be regarded as outstanding examples of faithfulness in service. It must be remembered, however, that while they were messengers of mercy on behalf of Lot and his two daughters, they were also ministers of vengeance, for were they not sent by God to witness the guilt of Sodom and punish it?

Committing our cares to Him, the Shepherd and Bishop of our souls, the "Angel of Jehovah" who preserved Lot, will keep every faithful follower from evil, to his eternal kingdom and glory.

He bids His angels pitch their tents
Round where His children dwell;

What ills their heavenly care prevents
No earthly tongue can tell! (Isaac Watts)

G. Jacob: Directed by Angels

" . . . The angel of God said to me in the dream, 'Jacob.' I answered, 'Here I am.' . . . 'I am the God of Bethel, where you anointed a pillar and where you made a vow to me. Now leave this land at once and go back to your native land.' " . . . Jacob also went on his way, and the angels of God met him. When Jacob saw them, he said, "This is the camp of God!" So he named that place Mahanaim. (Genesis 31:11, 13; 32:1)

Both on his flight from home and on his return to it, Jacob experienced intimate encounters with angels. At Luz, on the way to Padan-Aram, there was the dream of the ladder of ascending and descending angels (Genesis 28:12; John 1:51). The striking feature about the movement of the angels is that they were seen ascending from earth to heaven, then descending from heaven to earth, and not the other way round. These angelic guardians were round about lonely Jacob, making earth the very gate or vestibule of heaven (Genesis 28:17).

Jacob's mysterious ladder and the ministering angels represented more than divine providence. They symbolized Christ's triumphant work on man's behalf. Dr. Adam Clarke says,

It was probably a type of Christ, in whom the Divine and human nature are conjoined. The ladder was set up on the earth and the top of it reached to Heaven: for God was manifested in the flesh . . . Jesus Christ is the grand connecting medium between heaven and earth and between God and man. By Him, God comes down to man: through Him, man ascends to God.

Angelic guards surrounded Jacob and his family after the parting with Laban (Genesis 31:11–13); and as Jacob went on his way, the angels of God met him (Genesis 32:1). Assured of the protection of these celestial visitors, Jacob called the place *Mahanaim*, meaning "two hosts"—the angelic host and Jacob's own host of loved ones and flocks.

Jacob's wrestling with a person unknown, in the form of a man, whereby Jacob's name and nature were changed, savours of mystery. Hosea, however, unfolds a part of the mystery, declaring the stranger to be the *angel Jehovah,* the divine being who gave Jacob the name of Israel (Hosea 12:3–5). The same angel, who redeemed Jacob from all evil by a simple act of His sovereign will, changed the heart of Esau so that, when the brothers met, it was not in hate but love.

> Let Jacob's favoured race
> Adore with grateful love,
> The Living Way of truth and grace
> That leads to joy above.

> The way on earth is fixed:
> Its top the heaven conceals:
> Sinners and God it stands betwixt
> And God to man reveals.

> In duteous ministry
> Angels since time began
> Ascending and descending see,
> Upon the Son of Man!

> The ministerial host
> Their heavenly Lord attend;
> And us, who in His mercy trust,
> He bids his guards defend. (Charles Wesley)

H. Moses: Given the Law by Angels

. . . He was sent to be their ruler and deliverer by God himself, through the angel who appeared to him in the bush. . . . He was in the assembly in the desert, with the angel who spoke to him on Mount Sinai, and with our fathers; and he received living words to pass on to us. . . . You who have received the law that was put into effect through angels but have not obeyed it." (Acts 7:35, 38, 53)

... The law was put into effect through angels by a mediator. (Galatians 3:19)

For if the message spoken by the angels was binding . . . (Hebrews 2:2)

Sacred history abounds with the records of wonderful events in which angels had a share. Being God's ministers, angels were associated with the wonderful transaction of giving the law to Moses. The glorious Being who imparted the Ten Commandments and gave all the various directions and institutions to Moses was none other than the Second Person of the ever-blessed Trinity, whom Stephen called *The Angel.* The whole code of the law was mediated by Moses, the servant of God. (See chapter on "The Angel of the Covenant.")

Great numbers of angels attended the divine Majesty on Mount Sinai in the giving forth of His law (Deuteronomy 32:2; Psalm 68:17). They were there as ministering spirits of *The Angel Jehovah* and as witnesses of the momentous manifestation of His glory. The law was spoken by angels, which can mean that they delivered the law in articulate and audible sounds. When Moses died at the age of 120, the angel Michael buried him in an unknown grave in Moab (Deuteronomy 34:5–8; Jude 9).

I. Balaam: Reproved by an Angel

But God was very angry when he went, and the angel of the Lord stood in the road to oppose him. Balaam was riding on his donkey, and his two servants were with him. When the donkey saw the angel of the Lord standing in the road with a drawn sword in his hand, she turned off the road into a field. Balaam beat her to get her back on the road. (Numbers 22:22–23)

The soothsayer hired to curse Israel was a celebrity in the art of divination and guilty of gross hypocrisy in the service of God. Reproved by an angel and rebuked by an ass, Balaam learned the folly of cursing those God had blessed (Numbers 22:21–35). The angel who reproved this lover of the wages of unrighteousness (2 Peter 2:15) is referred to as an adversary, the Hebrew word for "adversary" being Satan (Numbers 22:22). This angelic reprover is not an evil spirit, not a created angel, but the uncreated one, the Angel of Jehovah's presence, that went before the people of Israel into the wilderness (Numbers 22:35). He was an "angel of mercy, who would have restrained Balaam from sinning and so was rather a friend than an adversary, had Balaam attended to him." A severe rebuke was administered by this angel. As Balaam ill-treated the ass, God gave a man's voice to the animal (Numbers 22:32–35).

Dr. Gill's commentary on this statement of the inspired historian is more to the purpose: he says,

> This was a very extraordinary and miraculous affair, and effected by a supernatural power, that a dumb creature which had not organs endued with speech, should speak so plainly and distinctly; and yet it should not be thought incredible: for what is [there] that Omnipotence cannot do?

J. Joshua: Encouraged by an Angel

> Now when Joshua was near Jericho, he looked up and saw a man standing in front of him with a drawn sword in his hand. Joshua went up to him and asked, "Are you for us or for our enemies?" "Neither," he replied, "but as commander of the army of the Lord I have now come." (Joshua 5:13–14)

Joshua, the faithful minister of Moses and his successor, was a prince of the tribe of Ephraim, and had a name meaning "salvation of God" (Numbers 13:8, 16). Conspicuous throughout his whole history were his mental endowments of a superior order; his courage, piety, wisdom, prudence and integrity—all gifts of the Spirit of God (Numbers 27:18–20; Deuteronomy 34:9).

Encamped in the plains of Jericho, Joshua awaited divine directions as to the actual possession of Canaan. While making a circuit of the strongly fortified city of Jericho, Joshua was confronted by the sudden appearance of a mysterious stranger, an angel who had come to assume command as "commander of the army of the Lord" (Joshua

5:13, 15). Recognizing the celestial character of this mysterious personage, Joshua acknowledged His superiority and divinity and awaited His commands. This angel-captain directed the siege of Jericho (Joshua 6:2–6).

John Owen, in his volumes on Hebrews, links this angel-warrior with the Captain of our salvation (Hebrews 2:10). Joshua worshipped the angel, which He accepted. Such worship was contrary to the duty and practice of created angels (Revelation 19:10; 22:8, 9).

K. Gideon: Commissioned by an Angel

The angel of the Lord went up from Gilgal to Bokim and said, "I brought you up out of Egypt and led you into the land that I swore to give to your forefathers. I said, 'I will never break my covenant with you, and you shall not make a covenant with the people of this land, but you shall break down their altars.' Yet you have disobeyed me. Why have you done this? Now therefore I tell you that I will not drive them out before you; they will be thorns in your sides and their gods will be a snare to you." When the angel of the Lord had spoken these things to all the Israelites, the people wept aloud . . . (Judges 2:1–4)

In the history of Israel the angels are represented as messengers of both wrath and mercy. They appeared to rebuke idolatry. Gideon was called by an angel to deliver Israel from her foes (Judges 6:11–21). While the angels ever have God in their thoughts, there is little doubt that the heavenly commissioner appearing to Gideon was the *Angel of the Covenant,* the *Lord of Angels.* (See chapter on "The Angel of the Covenant.")

While Gideon did not doubt the exalted character of the One he addressed as Lord, he yet ventured to ask for some visible token of His authority (Judges 6:17–18), which came in the eating of the meal Gideon prepared. Bishop Hall remarked, "Gideon intended a dinner, the angel turned it into a sacrifice." Wondering at the spiritual act he witnessed, Gideon lost sight of the agent (Judges 6:17–21). With all his fears removed by the Angel Jehovah, Gideon built an altar and called it "the Lord send peace" (Judges 6:22, 24).

L. Manoah: Instructed by an Angel

Manoah said to the angel of the Lord, "We would like you to stay until we prepare a young goat for you." The angel of the Lord replied, "Even though you detain me, I will not eat any of your food. But if you prepare a burnt offering, offer it to the Lord." (Manoah did not realize that it was the angel of the Lord.) Then Manoah inquired of the angel of the Lord, "What is your name, so that we may honor you when your word comes true?" He replied, "Why do you ask my name? It is beyond understanding." (Judges 13:15–18)

The birth and peculiar character of Samson were subjects of prophecy, delivered by "the Angel of the Lord" at a gloomy period in Israel's history. Manoah and his wife were godly people and desired a child, and their united prayer was heard in heaven and answered by a special messenger from God, as in the case of John the Baptist and also of Jesus Christ. The messenger appearing to Manoah was no ordinary angel, but the great Angel Jehovah, in whom he had perfect confidence. At first, regarding Him only as a man, Manoah offered Him suitable entertainment, but once conscious of His celestial dignity, both Manoah and his wife assured themselves of the authority of the One before them and of His right to the worship of their hearts and the sacrifice of their hands (Judges 13:22–23).

M. Israel: Chastened by Angels

So the Lord sent a plague on Israel from that morning until the end of the time designated, and seventy thousand of the people from Dan to Beersheba died. When the angel stretched out his hand to destroy Jerusalem, the Lord was grieved because of the calamity and said to the angel who was afflicting the people, "Enough! Withdraw your hand." The angel of the Lord was then at the threshing floor of Araunah the Jebusite. When David saw the angel who was striking down the people, he said to the Lord, "I am the one who has sinned and done wrong. These are but sheep. What have they done? Let your hand fall upon me a.. family." (2 Samuel 24:15–17)

As we are seeing, the angels of God were intimately associated with the trials and triumphs of the chosen people of God (Judges 2:1; Psalm 78:25, 49; Isaiah 63:9; Acts 2:4). At this point we are concerned with David's sin in numbering the people of Israel and with the punishment dispensed by an angel (see also 1 Chronicles 21), a punishment resulting in the destruction of 70,000 persons in three days.

David confessed his pride of heart and dependence upon the arm of flesh, and sought divine mercy, clothing himself in sackcloth and leaving the choice of chastisement to God. The angel who appeared to David, whose fearful ministry was so manifest, seems to have been the captain of the Lord's host. It may be that it was upon this occasion that David prayed:

> Who can discern his errors?
> Forgive my hidden faults.
> Keep your servant also from willful sins;
> may they not rule over me.
> Then will I be blameless,
> innocent of great transgression.
> May the words of my mouth
> and the meditation of my heart
> be pleasing in your sight,
> O Lord, my Rock and my Redeemer. (Psalm 19:12–14)

N. Elijah: Comforted and Translated by Angels

. . . he himself went a day's journey into the desert. He came to a broom tree, sat down under it and prayed that he might die. "I have had enough, Lord," he said. "Take my life; I am no better than my ancestors." Then he lay down under the tree and fell asleep. All at once an angel touched him and said, "Get up and eat." He looked around, and there by his head was a cake of bread baked over hot coals, and jar of water. He ate and drank and then lay down again. The angel of the Lord came back a second time and touched him and said, "Get up and eat, for the journey is too much for you." (1 Kings 19:4–7)

Twice over, the overwrought prophet was visited by an angel who prepared a meal for him and encouraged him on his way. It was also the angel of the Lord who inspired Elijah to courageously face the king of Samaria (2 Kings 1: 3, 15).

When the time came for Elijah to finish his extraordinary ministry, like Enoch before him, he did not taste death. He was translated. Having fought the wars of his God, Elijah was received by his God in a chariot of triumph with horses of fire—visible manifestations of angelic spirits. Gill says, "Angels are meant by chariots, and they are called chariots because they have appeared in such a form, and because, like chariots of war, they are the strength and protection of the Lord's people, and because of their swiftness in doing His work." (See 2 Kings 2:17; 6:17; Psalm 68:17, 18; Ezekiel 1: 4–13; 10:6.)

To Jordan's banks the chariot came,
While angels lined the road,
And bore the prophet wrapped in flame,
To his rewarding God. (Leeds)

O. Elisha: Defended by Angels

"Don't be afraid," the prophet answered. "Those who are with us are more than those who are with them." And Elisha prayed, "O Lord, open his eyes so he may see." Then the Lord opened the servant's eyes, and he looked and saw the hills full of horses and chariots of fire all around Elisha. (2 Kings 6:16–17)

Elisha, the disciple and successor of Elijah, was even more a miracle worker than his master. Elisha's pious wish that a double portion of Elijah's spirit might rest upon him was granted with the translation of Elijah. He witnessed angelic ministers, appearing like "a chariot of fire, and horses of fire." When, later on, profane youths of Bethel insulted Elisha by saying, "Go up, thou bald head! Go up, thou bald head!" they were saying in effect "Go up thyself to the pretended blessedness of immortality; follow thy master, Elijah, whom thou say is gone up to heaven by ministry of angels!"

Elisha's faith in the invisible angelic host surrounding and defending him came to be shared by his servant (2 Kings 6:13–17), whose eyes were opened by the Lord to discover that guardian defenders are more numerous than legions of spiritual foes. We, too, need the inner conviction regarding the invisible armies commissioned to guard God's servants when they are most exposed to danger. Elisha saw the mountains full of horses and chariots of fire—his servant saw only the Syrians, until the Lord opened his eyes.

> Thus the prophet's servant saw,
> When the Syrian host assailed,
> Every heavenly warrior,
> And bright encampment all unveiled.
>
> And from yonder distant sky,
> All conflict we shall view:
> Turn and see the dangers fly,
> And praise God that led us through. (Edmeston)

P. Isaiah: Commissioned by Angels

In the year that King Uzziah died, I saw the Lord seated on a throne, high and exalted, and the train of his robe filled the temple. Above him were seraphs, each with six wings: With two wings they covered their faces, with two they covered their feet, and with two they were flying. And they were calling to one another: "Holy, holy, holy is the Lord Almighty; the whole earth is full of his glory." At the sound of their voices the doorposts and thresholds shook and the temple was filled with smoke. (Isaiah 6:1–4)

The remarkable appearance of these two angels, seraphim, in the temple in Jerusalem, changed the life of the young prophet, Isaiah. Isaiah was grieving for his close friend, King Uzziah, who had died of leprosy. Jerusalem was in turmoil, the nation was in civil war, and an earthquake had devastated the city. The people were wealthy, but their hearts were cold toward God.

Then God sent two special angels, seraphim, each with six wings, to carry His call to a married man with two sons, the very gifted priest, Isaiah. As the angels spoke, the temple shook and was filled with smoke. Isaiah cried out, "*I am a man of unclean lips, and I dwell in the midst of a people of unclean lips. . . .*" The angel touched his lips with the live coal from the altar and said, ". . . *thine iniquity is taken away, and thy sin purged.*" Now cleansed, Isaiah heard the call of God, "*Whom shall I send, and who will go for us?*" He responded, "*Here am I; send me.*" (Isaiah 6, KJV)

After the visit of the angels, his cleansing and his call, Isaiah, in his next forty years, wrote with poetical genius the book which has been called "the climax of Hebrew literary art." He was also a great orator, speaking with conviction, until one day the wicked King Manasseh silenced the prophet's voice by having him sawn in two with a wooden saw (Hebrews 11:37). Now with the seraphim he rejoices in the presence of Jehovah. Sometimes the pen *is* mightier than the sword.

Q. Assyrians: Destroyed by an Angel

"O Lord, God of Israel, enthroned between the cherubim, you alone are God over all the kingdoms of the earth. You have made heaven and earth." . . . That night the angel of the Lord went out and put to death a hundred and eighty-five thousand men in the Assyrian camp. When the people got up the next morning—there were all the dead bodies! (2 Kings 19:15, 35)

The miraculous interposition of the angel in response to Hezekiah's prayer is another striking illustration of God's providential care. The defiant threats of godless Sennacherib did not trouble him. Hezekiah entreated God to interpose for preservation and to relieve any anxiety he may have had over the threats of the proud blasphemer of God; Isaiah was sent to assure the king of a speedy deliverance (Isaiah 37:16–20).

All God needed to crush the Assyrian army, 185,000 strong, was one angel (2 Kings 19:20, 21, 35). There are some writers who suggest that the "angel" mentioned here was a suffocating or pestilential wind, destroying the Assyrian army in a moment without noise, confusion, or any warning. We, however, believe that the agent responsible for such destruction was a celestial being, as in the case of the death of the first-born in Egypt (Exodus 12:29). If God is able to accomplish so much through one angel, think what He is able to do with a legion of angels (Matthew 26:53)!

R. Daniel: Ministered to by Angels

> Daniel answered, "O king, live forever! My God sent his angel, and he shut the mouths of the lions. They have not hurt me, because I was found innocent in his sight. Nor have I ever done any wrong before you, O king." (Daniel 6:21–22)

The prophet Daniel had no doubt as to the reality and service of angels. It was Gabriel, the archangel himself, who favoured Daniel with an exposition of the vision of the ram and the he-goat (Daniel 8:1–12). Gabriel was able to expound the vision of a divine prophecy. It was also Gabriel who again appeared on a mission of instruction and comfort and unfolded to Daniel the significance of the prophecies regarding the return of the Jews from Babylon, unto the coming of their Messiah (Daniel 9:3, 13, 19).

Daniel's three companions, refusing all homage to the senseless "golden image," faced a terrible death for their defiance of the edict of a godless monarch. But again, angelic comforters were at hand, ready to exhibit delegated power over fire and lions. The three Hebrew youths were preserved in the fiery furnace by One whose form was like unto the "Son of God" (Daniel 3:21–28, KJV).

The presidents and princes, excited by envy and jealousy, conspired to ruin the work of Daniel—but could not find cause to damage his character or his faith. For keeping his window open toward Jerusalem, Daniel was condemned to suffer. Thus into the lions' den he was thrown. But the God who created the lions was able to close their mouths. Daniel's guardian angel restrained the natural hunger of the ferocious brutes and gave the prophet a restful night.

S. Zechariah: Enlightened by Angels

Then the angel who was speaking to me said, "Proclaim this word: This is what the Lord Almighty says: 'I am very jealous for Jerusalem and Zion, but I am very angry with the nations that feel secure. I was only a little angry, but they added to the calamity.' Therefore, this is what the Lord says: 'I will return to Jerusalem with mercy, and there my house will be rebuilt. And the measuring line will be stretched out over Jerusalem,' declares the Lord Almighty. (Zechariah 1:14–16)

The series of visions granted to the prophet were fully explained by angels. We note:

1. Angelical reproof and predictions concerning the rebuilding of Jerusalem (Zechariah 1:16). The angel-man on the red horse was the Son of God, the same who had appeared to Joshua (Joshua 5:13, 14). Those who followed on red horses symbolized the angel-attendants of the Lord Messiah. Explanation of the vision was imparted by an angel (Zechariah 1:13–17).

2. Angelical predictions regarding the restoration of true religion in Jerusalem (Zechariah 3:1–6). Joshua, the Jewish priest, needed three things for his priestly office: pardon, purification and investment with holy robes, which the angel redeemer graciously afforded him.

3. Angelical predictions of the Messiah (Zechariah 3:6–8). The prophecy of the angel of the Lord is repeated and amplified in other parts of Zechariah (Zechariah 6:12–13). Messiah was promised, under the figure of a branch, sprouting from a tree, springing forth from the depressed but royal family of David.

The various references to angels in Zechariah prove they were God's ministers directing, guarding and watching over His subjects and empowered to carry out His designs. After four hundred silent years the prophecies were fulfilled. The angels announced, ". . . Unto you is born this day in the city of David a Saviour, which is Christ the Lord" (Luke 2:11, KJV).

7

The Angel of the Covenant

The angel of the covenant stands,
With His commission in His hand;
Sent from the father's milder throne
To make the great salvation known. (Isaac Watts)

"I will send my messenger, who will prepare the way before me. Then suddenly the Lord you are seeking will come to his temple; the messenger [angel] of the covenant, whom you desire, will come," says the Lord Almighty. (Malachi 3:1)

A. Introduction

There is in Scripture the manifestation of one angel who is distinguished from all others, who is not created, and who appears as the "Angel of the Lord God" (Genesis 16:7; Exodus 23:20; Judges 6:22, and others); the "Angel of His Presence" (Exodus 33:14); the "Captain of the Lord's Hosts" (Joshua 5:13–15); the "Angel of the Covenant" (Malachi 3:1); the "I AM" (Exodus 3:1, 6, 14). Under these various titles, this angel's name appears over forty times in the Old Testament. He is none other than the eternal Son Himself, who anticipates His incarnation and appears for the purpose of sustaining the faith and hope of His people, and of keeping before their minds the great redemption which was to take place in the fullness of time. Sometimes, indeed, it seems doubtful whether the "Divine Being" or a created angel is alluded to, but a study of the context will enable us to decide the question.

These appearances of Christ in the Old Testament are "theophanies" (derived from two Greek words, *theos* "God," and *pheino* "to appear"). This unique "Angel" of the Old Testament is the *Logos*, the Divine Word, the image of the invisible God who became God manifest in flesh (John 1:14). The truth is well expressed by John Calvin:

> For though he [Christ] was not yet clothed with flesh, he came down, so to speak, as an intermediary, in order to approach believers more intimately. Therefore this closer intercourse gave him the name of angel. (*Institutes,* p. 133)

B. His Appearance in the Garden

In the garden in the cool of the day, our first parents hid themselves from the Divine Presence amidst the covering of the trees. God called them from their hiding place, not only to pass the sentence of judgment, but, in mercy, to give the promise of a Redeemer. This *"voice of the Lord God,"* (Genesis 3:8, KJV) who came down to Paradise to wrest the victory from Satan's hands and to revive the hearts of the weeping pair, was none other than the Word of God, who came to remove the curse and to reveal the mercy of the Father by the gift of His Son (Genesis 3:15).

C. His Appearance to Hagar

Hagar, cruelly dealt with by Sarah, fled from Abraham's tent into the wilderness. The angel found her sad, solitary and homeless by a fountain of water. He spoke quietly to her and said, *"I will so increase your descendants that they will be too numerous to count"* (Genesis 16:10). Who can claim the power of creation, look into the future and foretell what will come to pass? Hagar recognized in the angel one greater than a created being, and said of the angel who spoke to her, "You are the God who sees me ... I have now seen the One who sees me" (Genesis 16:13).

D. His Appearance to Abraham

Abraham was sitting at the door of his tent in the heat of the burning noonday sun; three men appeared; he offered them hospitality. He did "*not forget to entertain strangers . . . angels without knowing it*" (Hebrews 13:2). One of the visitors stood out from the other two as chief in honor and greater rank. Then the Angel Jehovah said to Abraham, "*Sarah your wife will have a son. . . . is anything too hard for the Lord?*" (Genesis 18:10, 13). The same Angel, the Son of God, uttered a cry of mercy and grace at the offering up of Isaac (Genesis 22:11–13). Isaac himself received the promise of God from the Angel of the Lord (Genesis 26:2–5).

E. His Appearance to Moses

Moses, an exile from the Egyptian court, kept the flock of his father-in-law, Jethro, on the desert near Mt. Horeb. Suddenly one of the thorn trees of the desert was wrapped in flames, and yet the bush was not consumed. As he turned aside, he "*saw that though the bush was on fire; it did not burn up,*" and the Angel of the Lord said to him, " '*Do not come any closer.' Moses hid his face because he was afraid to look at God*" (Exodus 3:1–6).

F. His Appearance to Jacob

Jacob was highly honoured by the visitation of this divine messenger on leaving home (Genesis 28:3, 4), at Bethel (Genesis 28:10–22), at Peniel (Genesis 22:32), and at the end of his life (Genesis 48:15–16; Hosea 12: 4–5). The angel redeeming Jacob from all evil was no ordinary celestial messenger but the great Angel of the Covenant.

G. His Appearance to Joshua

In His office as the great Deliverer the same mysterious personage appeared to Joshua when he succeeded Moses as the leader of Israel

(Joshua 5:13–15). The "Captain of the Host of the Lord" required of Joshua the same tokens of adoration and worship as He did from Moses.

H. His Appearance to Manoah

The father of Samson was another honoured with a visit from this divine person, who appeared foretelling the birth and character of his extraordinary son (Judges 13:16–23).

I. His Appearance to Isaiah

Christ, in his pre-incarnation appearances to the prophets, came to them as the revealer of God. Both Isaiah and Ezekiel were granted a special manifestation of Jehovah and His glory at the time of their formal call to the prophetic office (Isaiah 6:1–13; Ezekiel 1:1–28). John tells us that Isaiah beheld Christ and His glory (John 12:39). The "words" and "burdens" Isaiah saw were communicated by Christ the speaker and sender. This "*Angel of Jehovah*" was Israel's Saviour (Isaiah 63:8–10). As "*the Angel of His Presence*," He revealed God. "*The Son is the radiance of God's glory and the exact representation of His being . . . For to which of the angels did God ever say, 'You are my son . . .'?*" (Hebrews 1:3, 5).

J. His Appearance to Zechariah

In many passages Zechariah describes a glorious person as intimately acquainted with the counsels of the Most High—as presiding over the affairs of the world: directing, vindicating and interceding, which ministry no ordinary angel could exercise (Zechariah 1:8–13; 2:8–11; 3:1–10; 6:12–15). In all instances cited, and others, the person described exhibits the attributes of omniscience and omnipresence and performs works only omnipotence could. This "*Angel of the Redeemer*," concerning whom it is written, "*My Name is in him*" (Exodus 23:21), uses the awesome formula by which the Deity confirmed the faith of those to whom revelations were given. He "*swears by Himself.*"

We heartily agree with Archbishop Magee that the Old Testament appearances of this divine person were appearances of, not "a mere angel, but God Himself." The unanimous opinion of all antiquity is that it was not the Father, but the Son.

K. Jesus Speaks about His Pre-incarnate Appearances

"Beginning with Moses and all the Prophets, he explained to them what was said in all the scriptures concerning himself." (Luke 24:27)

"If you believed Moses, you would believe me, for he wrote about me. But since you do not believe what he wrote, how are you going to believe what I say?" (John 5:46–47)

It was the greatest day in history! It was the first day of the week. As the sun rose, there was a great earthquake, and two angels came down from heaven. They looked like lightning, and the Roman soldiers collapsed like dead men. The Roman seal was broken, and the angels rolled back the huge stone to reveal the empty tomb of Jesus. To women standing by, the heavenly visitors announced, "*He is not here; He is risen.*" What a morning!

As the sun was setting that day, a second great event occurred. The risen Christ, while walking the long road from Jerusalem to Emmaus, approached two downcast disciples. They stood still, telling Him how they had believed that Jesus of Nazareth would be the one who would redeem Israel. Now he was dead, and his body had been stolen. Jesus replied by preaching one of the greatest expository sermons ever preached. "*Beginning with Moses and all the Prophets, he explained to them what was said in all the Scriptures concerning himself*" (Luke 24:27). He explained to them how the invisible God the Father was seen in His visible Son, as He appeared before His incarnation "*to Moses and the prophets*": He was the *Angel of the Lord* (Genesis 22:11–12), the *Angel of Jehovah* (Exodus 3:2), the *I am that I am* (Exodus 3:1, 6, 14), the *Captain of Hosts of the Lord* (Joshua 5:13–15), the *Angel of the Covenant* (Malachi 3:1). He no doubt concluded by quoting Malachi 3:1, " 'See, I will send my messenger, who will prepare the way before me. Then suddenly the Lord you are seeking will come to his temple; the messenger of the covenant, whom you desire, will come.' . . ."

Later the disciples said to each other, "*Wasn't your heart glowing while He was with us on the road, and when He made the Scriptures so plain to us?*" (Luke 24:32, Phillips).

L. A Final Word

How admirably adapted are these various but harmonious testimonies of the Old and New Testament to promote our spiritual edification! They invite, as they warrant, us to live by faith on the Son of God! Instructed thus, therefore, by the sacred scriptures concerning the Divinity and Messiahship of Jehovah Jesus, the Angel of the Covenant, the believer may rejoice that He will be with him or her. Almighty Guard, and quickened by the Holy Spirit, the Comforter, who glorifies the Saviour in the experience of all the faithful, every Christian may sing, to his or her daily peace and comfort. (Thomas Timpson, *Angels of God*, p. 210)

Arrayed in mortal flesh,
He like an Angel, stands,
And holds the promises
And pardons in his hands;
Commissioned from his Father's throne,
To make his grace to mortals known!

Should all the hosts of death,
And powers of hell unknown,
Put their most dreadful forms
Of rage and mischief on:
I shall be safe! for Christ displays
Superior power, and guardian grace! (Isaac Watts)

8

Angels in the New Testament

A. Introduction

The visits of the angels of heaven to the servants of G+od on earth appear to have been very few during the four hundred years between the time of Malachi and the long-awaited advent of the Messiah. From the close of the Old Covenant to the opening of the New Covenant, the chosen people of God suffered great oppressions, calamities and captivities. Many of the families became extinct; family records were thrown into confusion. Some were able to trace their lineage, especially the tribes of Levi and Judah. Thus the dying prophecy of Jacob held, "*The scepter will not depart from Judah, nor the ruler's staff from between his feet . . .*" (Genesis 49:10).

We should note that during the four hundred "silent" years the books of the Apocrypha were written. In classical Greek the word apocrypha means "hidden" or "concealed." Later it came to signify "the books that are obscure or hard to understand."

The study of angels in the Apocrypha is not our intent. However, our Roman Catholic readers find seven apocryphal books in their Bible. In the book of Tobit the angel *Raphael* comes to Tobiah, who has been attacked by a large fish. He tells Tobiah to remove the gall, heart, and liver to make "useful medicines." Tobiah does and is healed.

Our Jewish friends have thirteen apocryphal books. They identify the angel *Metatron* as the "Angel of the Lord" who is one with the *Messiah*. "The angels who serve the *Shechinah* are levels of archangels arranged in four groups before the throne of God. *Uriel's* group stands in front of the throne; *Raphael's* group behind it; *Michael's* group is to the right; and to the left is *Gabriel's*" (*Encyclopedia Judaica*, p. 974). Angels are everywhere in the New Testament. They are mentioned 184 times in seventeen books, by every author except James.

B. The Angel Gabriel Announces the Birth of John the Baptist

Once when Zechariah's division was on duty and he was serving as priest before God, he was chosen by lot, according to the custom of the priesthood, to go into the temple of the Lord and burn incense. . . . Then an angel of the Lord appeared to him, standing at the right side of the altar of incense. When Zechariah saw him, he was startled and was gripped with fear. But the angel said to him: "Do not be afraid, Zechariah; your prayer has been heard. Your wife Elizabeth will bear you a son, and you are to give him the name John." (Luke 1:8–9, 11–13)

Zechariah was of the priestly tribe of Levi; Elizabeth was a descendant of Aaron. Their exact ages are not known, some suppose she and her husband to have been about sixty years old. ". . . *They were both well along in years*" (Luke 1:7). As in the case of Abraham and Sarah, the birth of a son seemed impossible. With God, however, all things are possible. After eight hundred years of silence, Gabriel appeared in the fragrant smoke of the incense from the altar in the temple in Jerusalem, and said to the faithful priest Zechariah, "*Do not be afraid. . . your prayer has been heard. Your wife Elizabeth will bear you a son, and you are to give him the name John*" (Luke 1:13).

Elizabeth received various tokens of assurance. Her relative, the young virgin Mary, came all the way from Nazareth to Hebron to visit her. Together for about three months, they marveled at what the angel Gabriel had told them: that Mary had been chosen by God to cradle the Son of God, the Messiah, and Elizabeth to bring to the world John, the "*prophet of the Most High*" (Luke 1:76).

C. The Angel Gabriel Announces the Birth of Christ

In the sixth month, God sent the angel Gabriel to Nazareth, a town in Galilee, to a virgin pledged to be married to a man named Joseph, a descendant of David. The virgin's name was Mary. The angel went to her and said, "Greetings, you who are highly favored! The Lord is with you." . . . But the angel said to her, "Do not be afraid, Mary, you have found favor with God. You will be with child and give birth to a son, and you are to give him the name Jesus." (Luke 1:27–28, 30–31)

The memorable mission of Gabriel to the Virgin Mary is beautifully told by Luke the physician. The Gospels' record of the miracles, birth, ministry, death and resurrection of Christ testifies to the authenticity of Gabriel's prediction. Infinite wisdom arranged the whole plan for the advent of the great Messiah; but what do we behold in the circumstances of His birth? No palace or noble mansion was opened to receive the favoured pair, though they were of the royal family and signally honoured of heaven. They were poor; without means of procuring accommodations, even at the inn, which was too crowded to allow the privacy demanded by her delicate condition. The mother of the Son of Man, therefore, was reduced to the humiliating necessity of bringing forth her firstborn in a stable—that part of the inn or caravansary where the horses and cattle were penned—and of laying the mysterious babe for repose in a manger. Such were the accommodations of the "Lord of glory," when manifested in the flesh! Such was the condition determined in the everlasting covenant for the incarnation of the Son of God!

D. Christ and Angels

1. Incidents of the Ministry of Angels in the Life of Christ

a. Angels Announced to the Shepherds the Birth of Jesus

A multitude of the heavenly host chanted the honours of the birth of Jesus over the plains of Bethlehem (Luke 2:8–15). When the celestial choir returned to heaven, the fact of its appearance and anthem was spread abroad by the shepherds. It took angels to sing such Hallelujahs as those lowly men heard that day. Pious shepherds were the first to be privileged in hearing the joyful news, and that from angels of the court of heaven (Luke 8:21). The exalted society of angelic spirits, desiring to look into the things of Christ's birth, welcomed such an event with blissful admiration and with their heavenly songs.

> Hark! the herald angels sing,
> Glory to the new-born King!
> Glory in the highest heaven,
> Peace on earth, and man forgiven. (Charles Wesley)

b. An Angel Directed Joseph as to the Christ's Safety

When Joseph discovered Mary's condition, he must have been overwhelmed at what he perceived, and have sought direction, in his perplexity, from God. Graciously, God answered his cry through the ministry of an angel (Matthew 1:2–21, 24). Through the same angelic agency, Joseph was instructed to flee to Egypt and then, at a safe time, return (Matthew 2:13–20).

c. Angels Ministered to Christ after His Temptation

After our Lord's successful conflict with the Devil, angels placed themselves at His disposal, recognizing Him as Lord (Matthew 4:1–11; Mark 1:13). Of the mysterious events associated with the temptations of the prince of evil spirits and the succour afforded Christ by angels, Dr. Doddridge asks: "Who can read this account without amazement, when he compares the insolence and malice of the prince of darkness with the condescension and grace of the Son of God?"

It was a fourfold temptation! (1) To distrust—"*tell these stones to become bread*" (Matthew 4:3); (2) To presumption–"*throw yourself down*" (Matthew 4:6); (3) To worldly ambition—"*All this I will give you*" (Matthew 4:9); (4) To idolatry—"*if you will bow down and worship me*" (Matthew 4:9). Then, when the Devil reminded Jesus of the teaching of the Old Testament, he quoted scriptures—rather, he misquoted the text by leaving out the phrase "*in all your ways*" (Psalm 91:11), which spoke of the Lord's perfect dependence upon His Father's will (Hebrews 10:7, 9; Matthew 26:53).

Angels were not called in to assist in the grim encounter. Their assistance was not needed, for "*his own arm worked salvation for him*" (Isaiah 59:16). Once victory had been gained, however, the ministering spirits were on hand with the necessary supplies for the refreshment of His exhausted humanity. The original of "*angels ministered unto Him*" indicates, we are told, the spreading of a table for Him in the presence of His enemies, similar to the bread and water furnished by an angel for Elijah (1 Kings 19:5–8). The angels of God hovered around Jesus, and once Satan had been unmasked as a miserable, convicted fiend, the angelic companions and guardians were ready to succour their Lord, who had not eaten for forty days.

d. An Angel Strengthened Christ in His Agony at Gethsemane

While all four evangelists mention Christ's agony in the garden, it is Luke who adds three particulars unnoticed by the other three:

i. There appeared an angel from heaven strengthening Him.

ii. Being in agony, He prayed more earnestly.

iii. His sweat was, as it were, great drops of blood falling to the ground. "*An angel from heaven appeared to him and strengthened him. And being in anguish, he prayed more earnestly, and his sweat was like drops of blood falling to the ground.*" (Luke 22:43–44)

Divine inspiration alone can fully explain the adequate cause of Christ's amazing anguish. His Father, as the inexorable Judge, treated Christ not only as the Son of His love but as the surety for unnumbered millions of guilty creatures (Isaiah 53:1–12; Luke 24:46, 47; Hebrews 5:7–9).

> The Son of God in tears,
> Angels with wonder see;
> Be thou astonished, O my soul,
> He shed those tears for thee!

He wept that we might weep:
Each sin demands a tear:
In heaven alone no sin is found,
And there's no weeping there! (Author Unknown)

The appearance of a holy angel, as Christ was bearing a weight of
woe more than ten worlds could bear, encouraged His heart in such a
dark hour. In His humiliation He needed the assistance of an angel.
Being made "lower than the angels," He was capable of receiving help
from them. His friends slept as He agonized, but not the alert,
strengthening angel (Luke 22:43).

How did this special angel minister unto Jesus in His suffering?
Did he remind Him of the joy set before him? A writer, Matthew
Henry, suggests that:

"Perhaps *he did something to strengthen Christ,* wiped away His
sweat and tears, perhaps ministered some cordial to Him, or took
Him by the arm and bore Him up when He was ready to faint
away; and in these services of the angel, the Holy Spirit was *putting
strength into Him,* for so the word signifies."

It has been conjectured that the angel in the Garden was Gabriel,
whose name means the "mighty one" or "hero of God." This we do
know, Christ was "seen of angels" at His birth, His temptation and
now here in Gethsemane. The same elect angels are near to us, to guide
and guard, comfort and console.

e. Angels Were Witnesses and Heralds of Christ's Resurrection

An angel rolled away the stone at His tomb and announced the
resurrection to the women (Matthew 28:2–7). The angels who guarded
the tomb introduced the risen Lord to Mary Magdalene (John 20:11–14).
The testimony of what took place at the resurrection was rendered by
a vision of angels (Luke 24:23).

When Jesus stood in the place of sinners, bearing the load of a
guilty world, no angel appeared for His rescue or relief. But once He
had "made reconciliation for iniquity" and risen from the grave as One
who could not be held by death, celestial spirits announced His

resurrection unto life even as they had celebrated His entrance into life at His birth.

The Roman guards and all the formidable weapons of the Roman army were no match for an officer from the court of heaven. Vainly did the soldiers defend the sacred tomb of Jesus, for an angel rolled back the heavy stone from the door and made such an obstacle his seat (Matthew 28:2). This heavenly porter, in perfect composure as a servant in waiting, was ready to fulfill the orders of the risen Lord. Why should we fear obstacles when one angel was able to sit in ease, in defiance of the mighty legions of imperial Rome?

> Angels roll the rock away:
> Death yields up his mighty prey.
> Jesus, rising from the tomb,
> Scatters all its fearful gloom! (Dr. Gibbons)

The dazzling brightness of the angelic beings, which overcame the military guards, is also worthy of comment. The angel sitting on the stone had a countenance like lightning and raiment white as snow (Matthew 28:3, 4). It has been said that "lightning dressed in snow" is the only language able to describe the appearance of a heavenly inhabitant. The splendour of the world and its finest dresses are not worthy to be compared to the brilliant lustre of an angel clothed in his spotless robe.

> An emptied tomb with angels in it.
> Henceforth a place which angels use,
> To come and go with heavenly news. (Charles A. Fox)

f. Angels Attended Christ at His Ascension

During the forty days after His resurrection, our Lord gave His disciples infallible proofs of His victorious life (Acts 1:3). Then, when the time came for Him to ascend on high, He led His disciples out to Bethany (Luke 24:50). All at once the miracle happened, and Christ ascended on high (Luke 24:50, 51). While He ascended by His own divine power, we read that He was "carried up into heaven," a fact indicating that angels attended Him and formed His chariot, just as they did for Elijah when he was carried up in a chariot of fire to heaven (Psalm 68:17, 18; Acts 1:10–11). Of the angels, Gregg wrote:

> They brought His chariot from above,
> To bear Him to his throne;
> Spread their triumphant wings, and sang,
> "The glorious work is done!" (Gregg)

g. Angels Are to Attend Christ at His Second Advent

As Jesus ascended to heaven in a cloud of glory attended by a guard of mighty angels, so He is to descend to earth surrounded by myriads of these ministering spirits to assist Him in the execution of His holy work (1 Thessalonians 4:16; 2 Thessalonians 1:7, 9). If the appearance of one angel filled the guards at the tomb with such terror, how fearful will be the appearance of "ten thousand times ten thousand, and thousands of thousands" when they accompany the Almighty and Eternal King (Revelation 5:11, KJV)?

Everything related to Christ, then, is a matter of angelic inquiry (1 Peter 1:12). It is natural that angels should minister to Him in person and in a very intimate way, and their appearance with Him will proclaim the fruition of angelic hopes. The angels, who all through the centuries have been witnesses and sharers of His joy over repentant sinners, will be witnesses and sharers of the joy of the church when she is brought to her destined abode and is welcomed by her Bridegroom.

2. Summary of the Ministry of Angels in the Life of Christ
(Adapted from William George)

a. To foretell His conception (Luke 1:30–31)

b. To declare His birth (Luke 2:9–11)

c. To protect Him from danger (Matthew 2:13–14)

d. To minister unto Him in His need (Mark 1:13)

e. To protect Him from His enemies (Matthew 2:4, 13)

f. To comfort Him in His agony (Luke 22:43)

g. To open His grave (Matthew 28:2)

h. To witness to His resurrection (Luke 24:5–7)

i. To confirm His ascension (Acts 1:10–11)

j. To accompany Him to heaven (Ephesians 4:8)

k. To magnify Him in heaven (Revelation 5:11–12)

l. To reveal His will in heaven (Revelation 1:1; 22:16)

m. To fight for Him in heaven (Revelation 12:7)

n. To gather out those who offend Him (Matthew 13:49, 56)

o. To accompany Him at His coming (Mark 8:38; Matthew 25:31)

p. To execute His last judgment (Matthew 13:49–50)

3. Summary of Christ's Teaching concerning Angels

a. Their Solemn Task as Harvesters

. . . The weeds are the sons of the evil one, and the enemy who sows them is the devil. The harvest is the end of the age, and the harvesters are angels. (Matthew 13:38–39)

In His parable of the weeds Jesus taught the existence of a personal spiritual enemy of God and man, by whom evil is prompted in the world. ". . . *the enemy who sows them is the devil*" (Matthew 13:39). This is the one who is ever active sowing weeds—hard to distinguish from wheat in their earliest stages because of their resemblance to wheat—side by side with all God's wheat of truth and goodness. To pluck out weeds often means plucking up the wheat with them. God allows both to grow together until they are ripe, and when harvest comes at the end of the age, the angelic reapers will gather out all the offensive weeds and garner the wheat into God's storehouse (Matthew 13:41, 43).

". . . *The angels will come and separate the wicked from the righteous*" (Matthew 13:49). Mark put it that the angels will gather together the Lord's elect from "*the four winds*" (Mark 13:27). Theirs will be the solemn task of separating the wheat from the weeds. Our Lord's teaching, then, in the parable of the weeds, is patience and judgment. The *wheat* represents children of His kingdom, and the *weeds* children of the wicked one. Weeds and wheat grow up together. Then, as Richard Glover expresses it in *History of Jesus,* many like to try weed-grubbing— which requires more grace than man possesses:

> Pluck away hypocrites, and you will pluck up formal Christians who are not hypocrites along with them. Pluck up those "unsound" in doctrine, and you will pluck up some Christians who are travelling by paths of sincerest inquiry to the grandest views of truth.

Ours is the highest wisdom when, following the teaching of Jesus, we exercise a patience that leaves the separation of the weeds to the angels and the judgment of the deserved future of both the weeds and the wheat to the Saviour (Jude 15).

b. Their Guardianship of the Young

> See that you do not look down on one of these little ones. For I tell you that their angels in heaven always see the face of my Father in heaven. (Matthew 18:10)

One of the most precious aspects of our Lord's teaching about angels comes as the climax of His lesson to the disciples on the theme of humility (Matthew 18:1–14). This section has been called the "Magna Carta of workers among the young," as it expresses the truth of the blessedness of childhood and of the child-spirit. The object Jesus chose for His discourse was a little child—one old enough to be called, but young enough for Jesus to be "*taking him in his arms*" (Mark 9:36). Drawing attention to the child, Jesus registered His testimony against ambition by speaking as if two conversions were necessary for salvation: First, conversion *backward*: of the man into a child. Children have only to learn, not to unlearn; only to do, not to undo. Children easily enter the kingdom; pride keeps men from entering. Second, conversion *forward*: of the childlike man into a Christian—the daily crucifixion of pride of heart, so necessary because the passion to be great destroys the power to be great.

Then, unmasking the worldliness of ambition, declaring that everything heavenly must be free from the taint of pride, Jesus emphasized that the angels—children's angels, the guardian protectors, glad to stoop and take care of little ones—are free from injurious ambition. Jesus Himself was void of pride; mercy moved Him to lay aside the insignia of His majesty and come to save the perishing, and also "*the little ones*" (Matthew 18:10–14). Further, there is the underlying thought in what the Master taught that parents and teachers should seek the salvation of children and worthily discharge the office they share with the guardian angels (Matthew 18:14).

But what exactly did Jesus mean by His assertion, "*See that you do not look down on one of these little ones. For I tell you that their angels in heaven always see the face of my father in heaven*" (Matthew 18:10)? Do children have angels of their own? When they cease to be children, have they no further need of angelic guardianship? We do not feel that Jesus meant that each child born into the world is given in charge to some individual angel whose responsibility it is to watch over him or her and, in some way or other, render the child aid in the critical junctures of its life. The language Jesus used suggests that a certain company of angels *collectively* cares for children in general; the idea is that of *collective* rather than a *personal* or *particular* guardianship. Jesus did not say their *several* angels, but "*their angels,*" the plural "angels" favoring corporate rather than individual care. To the multitude of the children are assigned angels, many in number. These are heavenly beings, who "*see the face of my Father in heaven,*" which implies that they catch from the Father's face His love for little children and also their warrant to bring the saving truth into the mind of the child, and suggests that those who teach children should be in harmony with the angelic guardianship of the young.

Paul, however, reminds us that the care of angels is not confined to children. "*Are not all angels ministering spirits sent to serve those who will inherit salvation?*" (Hebrews 1:14). Just how they minister unto us, we are not told, but as they ministered to Jesus in the days of His flesh, so they undertake in unseen and unknown ways for the heirs of salvation, the redeemed of the Lord, whether they be young or old. Charles Kingsley uses the phrase, "the angels, ministers to God's elect." E. Young, writing of the way archangels and angels undertake for man, speaks of them as "sent by the Sovereign; and are these, O man, thy friends, thy warm allies?" An unknown poet would have us remember that "God sends great angels in our sore dismay; but little ones go in and out all day."

c. Their Likeness to Resurrected Saints

When the dead rise, they will neither marry or be given in marriage; they will be like the angels in heaven. (Mark 12:25)

Another saying of Jesus about angels is found in His answer to the Sadducee who came to Him in the temple with his carefully prepared difficulty of the woman who had had seven husbands and who wondered which out of the seven would be her husband in heaven. The reply of Jesus was uttered to point out the comparison or perfect the illustration: "At the resurrection people will neither marry nor be given in marriage; they will be like the angels in heaven" (Matthew 22:30).

What the Sadducee—who represented a sect that did not believe in resurrection—did not know was that conditions in the next world are not the same as here. Where there is no death, there is no need for the arrangements necessary here to keep the world populated. In heaven there is certainly love, but not marriage. All who are the sons of God are sons of the resurrection, and like unto the angels who neither marry nor are given in marriage. (See Luke 20:34–36.)

d. Their Joy over the Salvation of Sinners

. . . I tell you, there is rejoicing in the presence of the angels of God over one sinner who repents. (Luke 15:10)

The priceless teaching of Jesus about angels would not have been complete without His revelation that they share unbounded joy when sinners repent and turn to Jesus as Saviour. However lightly the conversion of a soul may be thought of among men, angels receive it with unbounded delight! Nothing so pleases them as the deliverance of a sinner from the power of darkness and his translation into the kingdom of God's dear Son. They do not originate the joy they express; it is *joy in their presence.* They share the joy of the Father, Son, and Holy Spirit.

"There is rejoicing in the presence of the angels of God over one sinner who repents." This picture occurs twice—at the end of the parable of the lost sheep and at the conclusion of the parable of the lost coin (Luke 15:7, 10)—but not, as we might have expected, at the end of the parable of the lost son. This parable does, however, conclude with the merriment and gladness of the father who, in his joy over the return of his prodigal boy, reflected the joy of heaven (Luke 15:32).

Then does not the language of Jesus seem to indicate that the angels are ever on the alert, marking what goes on in the sinner's heart, and delighting in every motion of repentance which they can detect? Latham asks, "If man can cause joy to the Angels of Heaven, can he dream of any goal of existence better worth reaching and more sufficing than this?"

No single angel takes the lead in rejoicing; the gladness caused by the repentance and salvation of the sinner is equally diffused; he is an object of interest to all the heavenly host. Angels share the joy of the shepherd who has recovered his lost sheep, and of the woman who has found her lost coin, and of the father whose son was lost but found again. Can we say that we share the joy of angels over sinners when we hear of them being gloriously saved by grace?

While angels sang with joy at the coming of the Redeemer, and now rejoice over those redeemed by His blood, they cannot sing the song of the redeemed, which is

A song unknown to angels' ears,
A song that tells of banished fears,
Of pardoned sins and dried-up tears.

e. Their Share in the Glory of Christ's Return

"For the Son of Man is going to come in his Father's glory with his angels . . ." (Matthew 16:27)

"No one knows about that day or hour, not even the angels in heaven . . ." (Matthew 24:36).

". . .when he comes in his glory and in the glory of the Father and of the holy angels." (Luke 9:26)

Often in His teaching about angels, Jesus spoke of them accompanying Him when He comes in the glory of His Father. Here, again, we have the truth of final separation—in His teaching on the judgment of the unprofitable and the reward of the profitable when all nations are gathered before Him. The figure is changed from weeds and wheat to sheep and goats. What a pregnant phrase that is, "He shall separate the people from one another" (Matthew 25:32)! In the mind of Jesus, there are only two classes: sheep and goats, saved and lost; and He alone is fit to be the judge of who should go to the right hand of honor and who to the left hand of shame.

When He comes in all His glory to sit upon the throne of His glory, "*the holy angels*" will form His retinue and assist Him in His judicial function. What prestige is to be the portion of His glory-clad attendants! Jesus declares their privilege of rank when He says, "*I tell you, whoever acknowledges me before men, the Son of Man will also acknowledge him before the angels of God*" (Luke 12:8–9). In His marvelous description of His coming "*. . . on the clouds of the sky, with power and great glory*" (Matthew 24:29–35), Jesus gave utterance to a phrase which has troubled theologians down the ages. As the Son of Man with His self-imposed human limitations, He was content to be without knowledge of the day of final judgment, even as the angels were. "*No one knows about that day or hour, not even the angels in heaven, nor the Son, but only the Father*" (Matthew 24:36, Mark 13:32). For us to fix dates is to falsify our position and contradict the clear teaching of Jesus. To quote Richard Glover:

> No day is named, that every day may be hallowed by the sense of the possibility of its being the day of his Advent. It helps to hallow each day of life, to realize that before its close we may be in the presence of Christ's glory.

E. An Angel Delivers the Apostles from Prison

But during the night an angel of the Lord opened the door of the jail and brought them [Peter and John] out. (Acts 5:19)

After the ascension of our Lord His followers, who constituted the first church, about 120 people, waited for the day of Pentecost. After the Holy Ghost came upon them, they began to speak in other tongues *"as the Spirit enabled them."* Then, by the power of the Spirit of God, they saw three thousand converts come to Christ in one day. As the infant church grew rapidly, so did the opposition of the bigoted priests, the infidel Sadducees, the court of the Sanhedrin, and those who arrested the apostles and put them in jail (Acts 5:18). That night, while Peter and John were sleeping in a dark, damp, filthy public prison, *". . . an angel of the Lord opened the doors of the jail and brought them out,"* and said, *". . . tell the people the full message of this new life"* (Acts 5:20).

> Prison, as we see, can offer no effectual impediment to ministering angels, in their services of love to the people of God; and it was, doubtless, with unutterable delight, that the celestial messenger obeyed the Divine commission to deliver the apostles, and encourage them in their ministry, even against the rulers of the nation, as they had dared to invade the prerogative of the Son of God. (Thomas Timpson)

F. An Angel Instructs Cornelius

At Caesarea there was man named Cornelius, a centurion in what was known as the Italian Regiment. He and all his family were devout and God-fearing; he gave generously to those in need and prayed to God regularly. One day at about three in the afternoon he had a vision. He distinctly saw an angel of God . . . (Acts 10:1–3)

The seaport of Caesarea was built by Herod and named in honour of Caesar. With marble docks, shining buildings, and a large 6,000 seat amphitheater (which is still standing), it was the Roman military capital of Palestine. There lived a man of great power, the soldier in charge, the centurion Cornelius. How did he come to know about God; why did he and his family pray daily? Why did an angel single out this Gentile for salvation? Could it be he had seen or heard Jesus? Many years ago an English missionary, Dr. Hales, wrote:

> . . . with much apparent probability that Cornelius had before been stationed at Jerusalem; and that it was he, commanding the

Roman soldiers who guarded the cross, witnessed the awful scene; they who had joined in the insults and mockeries of the whole cohort against Jesus in the pretorium so lately. For when the centurion who stood opposite to Jesus heard that he so cried and expired, with his last breath calling on God as his FATHER, he was fully persuaded that Jesus was indeed what he professed himself to be before the council, and said, "*This man was truly the Son of God*," Mar. xv. 39. The soldiers also, when they saw the earthquake, and the prodigies that happened, *feared greatly*, and joined in the same declaration with the centurion, "This was truly the *Son of God*," Matt. xxvii. 54. And again the centurion, when he saw the prodigy that happened, he *glorified God*, like a true convert, for this wondrous attestation of his Son's innocence, and said, "This man was really the *Just One*." Luke xxiii. 47 From the admirable character of this Roman, we are strongly inclined to suspect (though the conjecture is unwarranted by any of the commentators) that this was the *centurion* who attended Christ's crucifixion; and was evidently converted thereby. It was only *ten* years after. And he might have been permanently stationed at Caesarea, the seat of the Roman government. If so we can humbly see an appropriate reason why he should be so highly distinguished and honoured by God on this occasion, after having been a blasphemer and persecutor in ignorance, like Saul himself. To him, only, *an Angel* appeared, perhaps Gabriel.

Cornelius was not instructed in the mysteries of the gospel of Christ by the heavenly messenger, but only assured of acceptance with God, and directed how to obtain divine knowledge. He yielded a cheerful obedience to the commands of the angel; and accordingly, "*When the angel who spoke to him had gone, . . . called two of his servants and a devout soldier who was one of his attendants*" (Acts 10:7) to seek for Peter in the city of Joppa. Peter in response to the voice and the vision from God left Joppa for Caesarea, and stayed with the centurion and his family. As Peter preached to them the Holy Spirit came upon them, and they spoke in tongues and praised God, then were baptized by Peter. Thank God for that angel who was ready to go and bring to the Gentiles "*repentance unto life*" (Acts 11:18).

G. An Angel Releases Peter from Prison

The night before Herod was to bring him to trial, Peter was sleeping between two soldiers, bound with two chains, and sentries stood guard at the entrance. Suddenly an angel of the Lord appeared and a light shone in the cell. He struck Peter on the side and woke him up. "Quick, get up!" he said, and the chains fell off Peter's wrists. (Acts 12:6–7)

Peter's miraculous release from prison by the merciful mission of the angel of the Lord took place under peculiar and interesting circumstances; namely, at a remarkable period in the short history of the Church and of the Jewish nation under the brief reign of Herod Agrippa (Acts 11:19–21; 12:1–5). Herod courted popularity and, eager to gratify his subjects, sought to ruin the Christians. Thus Peter was apprehended and marked for execution after the Passover.

Peter's imprisonment and danger moved the Church to prayer. The saints knew they could do nothing against an unprincipled king, so they prayed without ceasing to their almighty Sovereign, who heard their petition and commissioned a mighty angel to effect Peter's immediate deliverance from prison and from the power of his enemies.

Is it not suggestive of God's goodness to Peter that He blessed him with sleep, for when the angel came to the apostle, he was *sleeping between two soldiers, bound with chains . . .*"? The prison doors were locked and bolted, yet the angel in some way paralyzed the military guards and caused the prison doors to open of their own accord. Hurriedly Peter found his way to the saints praying for his deliverance. But how amazed they were to see the answer to their prayers standing at the door! How guilty we are of asking, but not in faith believing! (Acts 12:12–16).

Herod, who anticipated the death of Peter, himself died most tragically, his sudden death being inflicted by the angel of the Lord because the monarch had failed to glorify God (Acts 12:20–23).

H. An Angel Instructs Philip

Now an angel of the Lord said to Philip, "Go south to the road—the desert road—that goes down from Jerusalem to Gaza." (Acts 8:26)

It was an angel who instructed the Roman soldier Cornelius in obtaining salvation; it was also an angel who led Philip to an Ethiopian in need of salvation. The angel marked out the road, then led him to the Gaza strip. The angel knew the wealthy Ethiopian's travel plans; the angel knew he was reading the book of Isaiah; the angel brought the evangelist and the seeker together. The Holy Spirit stepped in and encouraged Philip to preach Jesus, and the new Christian was baptized. Then the Spirit lifted Philip and took him to present-day Ashdod, thirty-four miles away. *In the same way, I tell you, there is rejoicing in the presence of the angels of God over one sinner who repents*" (Luke 15:10).

I. An Angel Sustains Paul in the Storm

"Last night an angel of the God whose I am and whom I serve stood beside me and said, 'Do not be afraid, Paul' . . ." (Acts 27:23)

The divine communication of the angel was intended to give credit to the Apostle Paul and to his doctrine, and to give him confidence when it appeared that every circumstance was against him. The fulfillment of the prediction that 276 passengers would be saved from shipwreck showed to the Romans and the other passengers that the God whom Paul loved and served would send His angel to guard and guide those who trust Him, and would save all for one man's sake.

The study of the ministry of angels in the New Testament would be incomplete without some consideration of the teaching of Paul concerning angels (IX), the teaching of the book of Hebrews concerning the superiority of Christ to angels (X); and the teaching of Revelation concerning angelic ministry (XI). These subjects we now consider.

J. The Teachings of Paul Concerning Angels

We now summarize Paul's teaching concerning angels as found in his epistles. The following are the principal features:

1. Angels Cannot Separate the Christian from the Love of God

For I am convinced that neither death nor life, neither angels nor demons, neither the present nor the future, nor any powers . . . will be able to separate us from the love of God, that is in Christ Jesus our Lord. (Romans 8:38–39)

Paul and all who stand with him are given "*overwhelming victory*" (Phillips) through Christ, whose love is stronger than death. Christ's power strips away the power of all potentially hostile forces. Christ is lord over all. No angel or any other created being can separate the Christian from God.

2. Angels as Spectators in the Work of Redemption

For it seems to me that God has put us apostles on display at the end of the procession, like men condemned to die in the arena. We have been made a spectacle to the whole universe, to angels as well as to men. (1 Corinthians 4:9)

Paul sees angels not only gazing upon the redeeming activities of Christ, the witness of the apostles and the Church, but also participating in the blessing of an increase of the manifold wisdom of God, made possible through the witness of believers throughout the world. We who believe are marching around the arena, on display before a sinful world, with our eyes on Him who leads the way.

3. Angels Will Be Judged by Christians

Do you not know that we will judge angels? How much more the things of this life! (1 Corinthians 6:3)

Paul has said that angels are the glorious associates of the Lord Jesus at His second coming; they collaborated in the giving of the Law; they were spectators of the ministry of redemption of Jesus Christ. Now for the first time he seems to reverse his position by stating, "Do you not know that we will judge angels?" Angels are not infallible beings (Job 4:18; 15:15). They have a moral responsibility and some day will be judged. Therefore, Paul is seeking to awaken the Church to its lofty position when on some future day "*we will judge angels.*"

4. Angels and Women

For this reason, and because of the angels, the woman ought to have a sign of authority on her head. (1 Corinthians 11:10)

This is one of the most discussed sayings of Paul. Some say that as angels are present when men and women gather to worship in the church or synagogue, women should have their heads covered with a veil or some other covering lest angels should be attracted by their charms (note Genesis 6:1). Others, however, point out that in Paul's day all married women were required to wear a veil on their heads as a sign that they were married. Therefore, a married woman should not grieve angels by the removal of her head covering, for this action would indicate she disregarded the ancient Jewish Law.

5. Angels and Tongues

If I speak in the tongues of men and of angels, but have not love, I am only a resounding gong or a clanging cymbal. (1 Corinthians 13:1)

It is assumed that angels use language in their communication with God and with each other, and perhaps various orders have their own dialects. Paul, when caught up into the third heaven, heard "*inexpressible*" words (2 Corinthians 12:4). Angels have modes of speech as well as man, but the nature of such angelic speech is nowhere discussed in the Bible.

6. Angelic Mediation in the Giving of the Law

What, then, was the purpose of the law? It was added because of transgressions until the Seed to whom the promise referred had come. The law was put into effect through angels by a mediator. (Galatians 3:19)

Paul declares that the Law was put into effect by angels. The statement that the Law was given by the mediation of angels appears also in Acts 7:53 and Hebrews 2:2. In Exodus nothing is said concerning the presence of angels in the giving of the Law. The Law is said to be given directly to Moses. However, there prevailed among the Jews of Paul's day the belief that angels were mediators of the Law; Paul accepts this tradition.

7. Angelic Hierarchies Were Created by Christ

For by him all things were created: things in heaven and on earth, visible and invisible, whether thrones or powers or rulers or authorities; all things were created by him and for him. (Colossians 1:16)

The New Testament teaches that Christ is outside creation, prior to it, distinct from it, and sovereign to all, for all things were created through Him and for Him. Angels are created beings; they are not independent beings; they are in no sense rivals to Christ or to those who are in Him. The rabbis of Colosse taught that there was one angel, *Metatron,* the greatest of all angelic princes, who stood next to the divine Ruler in honor. Paul wipes this teaching away by stating that Christ is Lord of all. Paul believed in the existence of angels and in their activities for Christ and for all who are hid in Him. "*He is . . . the Upholding Principle of the whole scheme of creation*" (Colossians 1:17, Phillips).

8. Angel Worship Is Forbidden

Do not let anyone who delights in false humility and the worship of angels disqualify you for the prize. Such a person goes into great detail about what he has seen, and his unspiritual mind puffs him up with idle notions. (Colossians 2:18)

The city of Colosse was associated with the cult of angel worship. Angels were placed in a position of mediation with regard to temporal and spiritual things. There was also the teaching that angels controlled the elements of the world. To the mind of Paul this imperiled the supreme lordship of Christ. He is the only mediator between God and man; He alone is worthy of all praise and honor.

9. Angels Partake in the Second Coming of Christ

According to the Lord's own word, we tell you that we who are still alive, who are left till the coming of the Lord, will certainly not precede those who have fallen asleep. For the Lord himself will come down from heaven, with a loud command, with the voice of the archangel and with the trumpet call of God, and the dead in Christ will rise first. (1 Thessalonians 4:15–16)

. . . and give relief to you who are troubled, and to us as well. This will happen when the Lord Jesus is revealed from heaven in blazing fire with his powerful angels. (2 Thessalonians 1:7)

Several times Jesus speaks of the activity of angels at the end of the world (Mark 13:27; Matthew 13:39, 49). He says, "*For the Son of man shall come in the glory of the Father with his angels . . .*" (Matthew 16:27, KJV). Paul asserts that the Lord Himself will descend "[1] *with a shout,* [2] *with the voice of the archangel,* and [3] *with the trump of God*" (1 Thessalonians 4:16, KJV). The archangel, according to Jewish tradition, is Michael (Jude 9; Revelation 12:7). When the Lord returns, His greatness and glory will be unveiled.

10. Elect Angels See Our Lives

I charge you, in the sight of God and Christ Jesus and the elect angels, to keep these instructions without partiality, and to do nothing out of favoritism. (1 Timothy 5:21)

As this is the only place in the Bible where "elect angels" are mentioned, it has called forth a large amount of discussion. Paul believed there are many ranks, or graduations, of angelic beings; here he mentions "elect angels." Who are they? The widely held view is that the elect angels are those who retained their purity and obedience when certain of the angels fell. They are the angels who kept "*their position of authority*" and did not "*abandon their own home*" (Jude 6).

K. The Teachings of the Book of Hebrews on Angels

So he became as much superior to the angels as the name he has inherited is superior to theirs. For to which of the angels did God ever say, "You are my Son; today I have become your Father"? (Hebrews 1:4–5)

The book of Hebrews was written to Jews in order to convince them of the truth that (1) Christ is superior to angels: (2) Christ is superior to Moses; (3) Christ is superior to Aaron. Here we consider the first proposition, that Christ is superior to angels.

It may be questioned why such an obvious comparison should have to made, for there can be no question of Christ's superiority over angels. Before His incarnation He was higher than the angels, but in His human form He was made lower than the angels: *You made him a little lower than the angels; . . . But we see Jesus, who was made a little lower than the angels . . .* (Hebrews 2:7, 9). Now, as before His incarnation, He is again higher than the angels.

Angels were venerated by the devout Jews. The angels gave them the Law through Moses; angels ministered to Abraham, Jacob, Joshua, and Elijah. Angels led them through the forty-year journey in the wilderness, and cherubim watched over the ark of the covenant. Thus it was essential that the Jewish believers should understand the infinite superiority of Christ over the heavenly beings they reverenced in their lives. If the law that was given by angels could not be slighted, how could men and women escape condemnation if they neglected the word spoken by One who is infinitely superior in design and power to angels—even the Lord Himself?

Therefore Christ is shown in Hebrews to be greater than angels in the following ways: (1) Because He has a more excellent name than they (1:4–5), (2) Because angels of God adore Him (1:6), (3) Because angels were created by Him (1:7), (4) Because in His human nature He had greater gifts than angels (1:8–9), (5) Because He is eternal (1:10–12), (6) Because angels are servants of God; He is the Son (1:14), and (7) Because He subdued all things (2:9).

Therefore God exalted him to the highest place and gave him the name that is above every name, that at the name of Jesus every knee should bow, in heaven and on earth . . . (Philippians 2:9–10).

L. Angelic Ministry in the Revelation of John

"I, Jesus, have sent my angel to give you this testimony . . ."
(Revelation 22:16)

How he, who lone on Patmos banished,
Saw in the sun a mighty angel stand;
And heard great Babylon's doom pronounc'd by
Heaven's command. (Robert Burns)

After the death of the Apostle Paul, the church which he founded
in Ephesus invited the Apostle John, the cousin of Jesus, to be their
pastor. He accepted. However, about 95 AD, under the persecution of
Domitian, the aged John was sent in chains from Ephesus to the
remote island of Patmos to work in the mines. Tradition says that the
natives of Patmos received him and his scribe with respect. John
preached in the marketplace; he performed miracles; he baptized
those who believed. In appreciation the natives provided a cool, two-
room cave for John and his scribe.

One day, after John had been in prayer and fasting for twenty days,
. . . "On the Lord's Day I was in the Spirit, and I heard behind me a
loud voice like a trumpet, which said: 'Write on a scroll what you see
. . .'" (Revelation 1:10–11). Thus we have the book of Revelation, or
the Apocalypse, the unveiling of things which up to that time were
known only to God. The simplest outline of the book is that suggested
by Dr. G. Campbell Morgan: (I) The Glory of Christ, chapter 1;
(II) The Grace of Christ, chapters 2–3; (III) The Government of
Christ, chapters 4–22.

As we open and read the book of Revelation, chapters 5–10 describe powerful angels, with great wisdom, judging the wicked nations. In the closing chapters, Revelation 21–22, joyful angels in the
new heaven join in adoration and praise to the Lamb of God and His
bride, the church. Adam Clarke, the great expositor, after spending
thirty years working on his commentary of the Bible, finally came to
the book of Revelation. In his preface to the book he wrote,

I had resolved for considerable time, not to meddle in this book,
for I saw that I would produce nothing satisfactory on it; but when

I reflected that the literal sense and phraseology might be made plainer by the additional critical notes . . . I changed my resolution and have added short notes principle philological where I thought I understood the meaning. (*Commentary on Revelation of St. John*, "Preface," p. 966)

J. B. Phillips, in the preface of his translation of the Apocalypse, states:

I was naturally tempted to omit the book altogether from my translation work, incidentally taken by Calvin in his New Testament commentary . . . Yet after much study I became satisfied that the Christian Church was justified in including this book in the Sacred Canon . . . For in this book the translator is carried, not into some never-never land of fancy, but into the ever-ever land of God's eternal Values and Judgments. (*The Book of Revelation*, "Preface," p. ix)

This has been our struggle: "Why touch Revelation?" I then came to realize this book must be included, for it is the "angel book" of the New Testament. The glorious angels of our righteous God are everywhere in the last book of the Bible. They are mentioned seventy-seven times. They are described as: holding back the winds, looking like stars, standing in the presence of God, flying like eagles, appearing like living creatures, sounding golden trumpets, numbering the tribes of Israel, proclaiming the eternal gospel, opening seals, pronouncing judgment on Babylon and the Roman Empire, delivering messages to the churches, singing hallelujah, holding the chains to bind Satan, measuring the new Jerusalem, sitting at the twelve gates of the new city, and taking John on a tour along the banks of the "*. . . river of the water of life, as clear as crystal, flowing from the throne of God and of the Lamb . . .*" (Revelation 22:1).

We now consider selected, self-explanatory last words of angels as recorded by John for our instruction and edification:

"Holy, holy, holy is the Lord God Almighty, who was, and is, and is to come" (Revelation 4:8).

"Worthy is the Lamb, who was slain, to receive power and wealth and wisdom and strength and honor and glory and praise!" (Revelation 5:12).

"Come! . . . Come! . . . Come!" (Revelation 6:1, 3, 5).

"Amen! Praise and glory and wisdom and thanks and honor and power and strength be to our God for ever and ever. Amen!" (Revelation 7:12).

"Woe! Woe! Woe . . ." (Revelation 8:13).

Then I heard a voice from heaven say, "Write: Blessed are the dead who die in the Lord from now on." "Yes," says the Spirit, "they will rest from their labor, for their deeds will follow them" (Revelation 14:13).

They held harps given them by God and sang the song of Moses the servant of God and the song of the Lamb: "Great and marvelous are your deeds, Lord God Almighty. Just and true are your ways, King of the ages" (Revelation 15:2–3).

"Yes, Lord God Almighty, true and just are your judgments" (Revelation 16:7).

Then the angel said to me, "Write: 'Blessed are those who are invited to the wedding supper of the Lamb!' " And he added, "These are the true words of God" (Revelation 19:9).

I heard a loud voice from the throne saying, ". . . He will wipe every tear from their eyes. There will be no more death or mourning or crying or pain, for the old order . . . has passed away" (Revelation 21:4).

. . . I fell down to worship at the feet of the angel who had been showing them [these things] to me. But he said to me, "Do not do it! I am a fellow servant with you . . . and of all who keep the words of this book. Worship God" (Revelation 22:9).

The last words of angels in the Bible reveal that there is little, or no, time for the wicked to repent when death comes, or Christ returns. It is too late to change: they will "continue in [their] wickedness." Those who have accepted the good news must continue in good deeds, and they will in eternity "continue in . . . holiness." "Do not seal up the words of the prophecy in this book, for the time of their fulfillment is near. Let the wicked man continue his wickedness and the filthy man his filthiness; let the good man continue his good deeds and the holy man continue in holiness" (Revelation 22:11, Phillips). Jesus said, "The harvest is the end of this world. The reapers are angels. . . . the good will shine out like the sun in their Father's Kingdom. The man who has ears should use them!" (Matthew 13:39, 43, Phillips).

Conclusion

There is a new wave of interest in angels in our land today. Public interest is evidenced by the many books, magazine articles, and stories of angel encounters or near death experiences. Movies and television shows feature shining angel companions. People need protection; people are searching for a more meaningful life; people are looking for deeper spirituality. This interest in angels reveals the longing of the human inner life to have contact with angels.

When *Time* magazine in their extensive poll asked, "Do you believe in angels?" sixty-nine percent of those answering said "yes." When asked, "Have you personally felt an angelic presence?" thirty-two percent responded "yes." A survey among Roman Catholic and Protestant church members revealed that ninety-seven percent believe in angels, and twenty-three percent have seen angels. The angels were seen in dreams or in a bright human or angelic form.

Angels do not change; they are ever the same. They can do for those who believe today what they accomplished in times past. Billy Graham says, "Every true believer in Christ should be encouraged and strengthened! Angels are watching; they mark our path. They superintend the events of your life and protect the interests of the Lord God, always working to promote His plans and to bring about His highest will for you."

As Europe emerged from the Dark Ages, a leader of the Reformation, John Calvin, wrote, "Scripture informs us that angels guard our safety, undertake our defense, direct our way, and exercise constant solicitude that no evil befalls us . . . all orders of the celestial army watch for our safety . . . not one particular angel" (Book 1, Chapter 14).

In every age, old and new, the Bible reveals all that we need to know—all that our finite minds can comprehend—about angels. The sacred Scriptures of Jews, Catholics, and Protestants develop the doctrine of angelology, which rests not upon reason or supposition, but upon revelation. "As the universe has been ordered, it has not pleased God to give more intercourse with the angels or any consciousness of their presence; yet the Bible states that angels not only observe the affairs of men, but that good angels minister to man's well-being (Hebrews 1:14)" (Lewis Sperry Chafer, Book 2, Page 3).

In our study of *All the Angels in the Bible* we have read that angels exist as the eternal messengers of Yahweh and also as the companions of the church and Christians. These angelic beings are God's powerful attendants, and also the keepers of those who follow Christ. They have *strength* in the one hand, in the other *tenderness*.

Their strength is illustrated in the shutting of the mouths of lions, the slaying of 185,000 Assyrians, the rolling away of the sealed stone at the tomb of Jesus, and the winning of the final war in heaven against the devil and his fallen angels. Their tenderness is illustrated in their provision of water for Hagar in the desert, a sacrifice for Abraham, food for Elijah, a dream for Jacob, good news for the shepherds, a miracle for Mary and Joseph and strength for our suffering Saviour.

Let us not be afraid of the evil within or the evil without. God has ordained His angels of strength and tenderness who will minister to our daily needs as we come in prayer, in faith, in the name of the Father, Son, and Holy Spirit. We do not have to wait to die to encounter the strength and the tenderness of angels. "*Are not all angels ministering spirits sent to serve those who will inherit salvation?*" (Hebrews 1:14). Angels are part of our daily lives: night and day they are near; sometimes we see or feel their presence; on occasion they save us from danger; sometimes they touch our tired and weak bodies; sometimes we entertain angels without knowing it (Hebrews 13:2). Angels today hear our prayers; they know when we give to the poor; they guard us in danger; they are there when we are afraid; they watch over our children; they know when we acknowledge Christ; they know when we disown Christ; they are with us when we die; they will meet us in heaven; they are offended if we worship them. Some day we will judge them for their faithfulness to God, to the Lord Jesus, and to us who believe.

This leads to some final words of conclusion:

> The challenge of the study of angels is today, as always, that of claiming their theological significance for the church and the proclamation of the Gospel. If, like the pointed finger, angels direct our attention to themselves, then they lead the faithful astray, and their end becomes worse than either the denial of their existence or their non-existence. The task of the faithful and the church is to reclaim them as messengers *of God,* to assay their role in the economy of salvation, to investigate their employment in the Divine purpose, and to recognize anew how they become vehicles of the grace of God that comes to the world in Jesus Christ. When angels are perceived and received as messengers *of God,* then their obedience to the divine becomes a source of inspiration for our obedience to it; the purity of their worship and praise of God assists us in our feeble efforts in the same; and their assistance in times of adversity and discouragement enables us to know that we are not alone in our earthly pilgrimage of faith, but that God is the lover of our souls who declares Himself to be our Guide, Protector, and Savior. (Contributed by James R. Edwards, Jamestown College, 1995.)

> Therefore, whatever is said concerning the ministry of angels, let us direct it to this end, that, overcoming all diffidence, our hope in God may be more firmly established. For the Lord has provided these guards for us, that we may not be terrified by a multitude of enemies, as though they could prevail in opposition to His assistance, but have recourse to the sentiment expressed by Elisha, "There are far more for us than against us (2 Kings 6:17)." (John Calvin, *Institutes of the Christian Religion,* Book 1, Chapter 12, p. 160)

> Lord! when I leave this mortal ground,
> And Thou shalt bid me rise and come,
> Send a beloved angel down,
> Safe to convey my spirit home! (Isaac Watts)

SECTION THREE

■   ■   ■

Compendium of Angels

Questions and Answers about Angels

Q: Do angels have wings?

A: The *seraphim* are represented as having six wings (Isaiah 6:1, 6). The *cherubim* have four wings (Ezekiel 1:11). Each of the four *living creatures* had six wings (Revelation 4:8). Angels often appear as men with or without splendour or wings, yet can move at the speed of light.

Q: Were angels created?

A: Yes. They were created by God (Psalm 148:1–5; Colossians 1:16). "*For by him all things were created: things in heaven and on earth.*"

Q: Does the Bible teach the existence of guardian angels?

A: Yes. Although the Bible does not use the expression "guardian angels," we believe angels are sent to guard us. "*For he will command his angels concerning you to guard you in all your ways*" (Psalm 91:11). Also they watch over children: "*. . . do not look down on one of these little ones. For I tell you that their angels in heaven always see the face of my Father . . .*" (Matthew 18:10).

Q: If God created angels, how could they sin?

A: God created *man*; and man sinned and was banished from the Garden of Eden (Genesis 3:24). God created *Satan,* and he sinned (Isaiah 14:12). God created the *angels,* and some have sinned (2 Peter 2:4). Men and angels have free will. The Lord Jesus Christ through His death provides redemption for mankind (John 3:16; Romans 6:23). The *devil* and his fallen angels have no redemption. However, they are still angels: they are incorruptible and are immune to human discomfort; but in the end they will be banished and tormented day and night forever (Revelation 20:10).

Q: Is it possible for angels to fall today?

A: There is nothing in Scripture which would indicate that angels can fall today. Their fall was before the creation of the world as recorded in Genesis 1:2. Evidently the angels today are confirmed in their position and, therefore, cannot fall any more. Exactly *when* Satan and his angels rebelled, through pride and envy, against their Creator is known only to them. God in His sovereignty gave to angels and men the choice of good and evil. If we can win the prize of heaven, we can also lose it.

Q: Who are the "sons of God" in Genesis 6:2?

A: This is a very difficult question. Theologians, commentators, and Bible students do not agree on the meaning of this verse. There are three principal answers to this question: (1) According to the *Targums,* chief Jewish expositions, they were nobles of men of highest rank. (2) They were angels. Ephesians 2:4, 2 Peter 2:4, and Jude 6 seem to favor this interpretation, but a high authority has said, "*angels neither marry nor are given in marriage.*" (3) The most generally accepted interpretation is that the sons of *Elohim* were Sethites, and when they married for mere lust of beauty, universal corruption ensued (Lang's *Commentary,* Volume 1, page 35). M. R. DeHaan, however, says that "when the Bible states that angels in heaven neither 'marry nor are given in marriage,' one must remember that this is spoken of as angels of God in heaven, while those in Genesis 6:1 are not in heaven, but are fallen angels."

The account of the mating of the sons of God with the daughters of men in Genesis 6:1–4 is unique in the Bible. No other passage of Scripture relates or even hints at members of the celestial world having sexual intercourse with human beings. "By an act of rebellion a new level in the spread of evil is attained, to which divine judgment is the only antidote . . . So the Lord said, 'I will blot out man whom I have created' (Genesis 6:5, 7). Noah is immediately introduced, and the story of the flood commences" (J. R. Edwards). ". . . Some fallen angels transgressed not only by taking on human bodies—as we know fallen angels sometimes do—but by operating in all the functions of those bodies, including sex." (Terry Law, *The Truth about Angels*, p. 223) Our conviction is that sin reached its climax in the illicit intercourse between fallen angels and women.

Q: Why did God not destroy the devil when he sinned?

A: In answer to this we can only point to Deuteronomy 29:29: "*The secret things belong to the Lord our God, but the things revealed belong to us and to our children . . .*" God is not required to give us an answer for what He does. He is sovereign and the master of all His creation. Someday we will understand; now we accept and believe. In the end of this age Satan will be bound forever and ever (Revelation 20:10).

Q: Can the existence of angels be proved by the "chain of being" theory?

A: The great "chain of being" theory can be regarded either as a philosophical doctrine concerning the layout of nature or as a theological doctrine concerning the design of a universe created by God. The second of these two ways provides the "theological explanation of why God created angels" (Martin F. Adler, *The Angels Among Us*, page 59).

Paul says that even in this world not all flesh is identical. There is a different flesh of human beings, animals, fish, and birds (1 Corinthians 15:39, Phillips). All nature seems to be linked together in gradual order. The chain begins from the vegetable and works its way up through plants, insects, animals, fish, and birds, to human beings. Because the gap between God and humans is so great, our reason dictates there must necessarily be high orders of angelic intelligences such as cherubim, seraphim, archangels, and angels of all ranks in the "chain of being."

> "When we consider the infinite power and wisdom of the Maker, we have every reason to think . . . that the species of creatures should also, by gentle degrees, ascend upwards from us to infinite

perfection, as we see them gradually descend from us downward."
(John Locke)

Q: Can we contact angels?
A: Yes. Jesus said to the companion who sought to protect Him
from the soldiers of the high priest, "*Put your sword back in its place . . .
Do you think I cannot call on my Father, and he will . . . put at my
disposal more than twelve legions of angels?*" (Matthew 26:52–53).
It is the Father in heaven who hears our cry for help, who commands
His waiting angels to contact us. We can only contact angels through
Him. They are His messengers, His servants, not ours unless He
commands.

We read in the Old Testament of Hagar's little son Ishmael crying, as
he was dying of thirst in the parched desert. "*God heard the boy crying
and the angel of God called to Hagar from Heaven and said to her, ' . . .
Do not be afraid. . .' Then God opened her eyes and she saw a well of
water. . .*" (Genesis 21:17,19). She did not ask an angel to help her. God
heard her cry for help, and He sent His angel.

Believers are indwelt by the Holy Spirit. This gives to us a spiritual
nature, and through prayer, meditation, and study of the word of God
we make our needs known to our heavenly Father. He will send His
angels to contact us—to confront, strengthen, and protect us. Some
encounters we will be able to describe; some will not be known until
the mists of earth have rolled away.

> He will command his angels concerning you,
> to guard you in all your ways;
> they will lift you up in their hands,
> so that you will not strike your foot against a stone. (Psalm
> 91:11–12; see also Luke 4:10–11)

Study Questions on Angels

This book, in conjunction with these study questions and the Scripture references, can be used as an eight-week study class in "All the Angels of the Bible."

Suggested division of the material:
Week One: Questions 1 and 2
Week Two: Questions 2 and 3
Week Three: Questions 4 and 5
Week Four: Question 6
Week Five: Question 7
Week Six: Question 8
Week Seven: Questions 9 and 10
Week Eight: Question 11

Class Study Questions

1. What can we learn from the Bible about the creation and abode of angels?
    A. When were the angels created?
        Job 38:1–4
        Nehemiah 9:6
        Colossians 1:16
    B. What do angels look like?
        Job 38:4–6
        Daniel 10:1–18
        Ezekiel 24:9–10

2. Explain the "spiritual bodies" of angels.
    A. What do we mean by "ministering spirits"?
        1 Corinthians 15:39
        Hebrews 1:14
    B. How do angels differ from God?
        Judges 13:18–19
        Colossians 1:16–17
3. Where do angels live?
    A. What do we mean by "the third heaven"?
        2 Corinthians 12:2
        Jude 9
    B. Can we distinguish one heaven from another?
        Genesis 1:26
        Isaiah 13:10
        Revelation 4:7
4. Does the Bible give the number of angels?
    A. Are there many or few?
        Daniel 7:10
        Matthew 26:23
        Revelation 5:11
    B. Explain what John saw on the Isle of Patmos.
        Revelation 1:3–9
5. Are angels given names and titles? Explain.
    Gabriel
        Daniel 8:16–27; 9:21; Luke 1:19, 26–35
    Michael
        1 Thessalonians 4:16
    Seraphim
        Isaiah 6:2–6
    Cherubim
        Ezekiel 1:5–18; 10:12
    gods
        Psalm 97:7; Job 38:7
    Watchers
        Daniel 4:13, 17, 23
    Powers
        Ephesians 6:12; Colossians 1:6

6. Describe the different ministries of angels to men and women in the Old Testament.

Adam and Eve
    Genesis 3:24
Abraham
    Genesis 22:18
Hagar
    Genesis 21:17–18
Eliezer
    Genesis 24:7
Lot
    Genesis 19:15–16
Jacob
    Genesis 32:1–2
Moses
    Deuteronomy 32:2; Hebrews 2:2
Balaam
    Numbers 22:22–23
Joshua
    Joshua 5:13–14
Gideon
    Judges 2:1–4
Manoah
    Judges 13:15–18
Israel
    2 Samuel 24:15–17
Elijah
    1 Kings 19:4–7
Elisha
    2 Kings 6:16–17
Isaiah
    Isaiah 6:1–8
Assyrians
    2 Kings 19:15, 35
Daniel
    Daniel 6:21–22

Zechariah
    Zechariah 1:14–16
7. Explain the unique appearances of the Angel of the Covenant.
    A. Who is He?
    Malachi 3:1
    B. Discuss His appearances to the following:
    Adam and Eve
        Genesis 7:13
    Hagar
        Genesis 16:13
    Moses
        Exodus 3:1–6
    Abraham
        Genesis 18:10–13
    Jacob
        Genesis 32:2–32
    Joshua
        Joshua 5:13–15
    Manoah
        Judges 13:16–23
    Isaiah
        Isaiah 6:1–13; John 12:39
    Zechariah
        Exodus 23:2–3; Zechariah 1:8–13
    C. Did Jesus say He appeared in the Old Testament? Explain.
    Luke 24:27
    John 5:46–47
8. Describe and discuss the appearances of angels in New Testament times.
    Zechariah
        Luke 1:8–9
    Virgin Mary
        Luke 1:27–31
    At His birth
        Luke 2:8–15
    As a child
        Matthew 2:2, 21, 24

In the wilderness
    Matthew 4:1–11
In Gethsemane
    Luke 22:39–46
The resurrection
    Matthew 28:2, 7; Luke 24:23
His ascension
    Luke 24:50–51
His return
    1 Thessalonians 4:16; 2 Thessalonians 1:7–9
Peter
    Acts 5:19–20
Cornelius
    Acts 10:1–3
Philip
    Acts 8:1–40
Paul
    Acts 27:13–14
John
    Revelation 1:1

9. What does Paul say about angels? Follow the chapters and discuss these Scriptures:
    Romans 8:38
    1 Corinthians 4:19; 6:3; 11:9; 13:1
    Galatians 3:19
    Colossians 1:16; 2:18
    1 Thessalonians 4:15–16
    2 Thessalonians 1:7
    1 Timothy 5:21

10. What does the book of Hebrews teach about Christ and angels? Christ is better than angels. See: Hebrews 1:4–14; 2:9. Also see section on Hebrews.

11. What does the book of Revelation teach about angels? See section on Revelation.

Every Reference to Angels
in the Bible

Bible References to a Single Angel (207)

The angel of the Lord found Hagar near a spring in the desert; it was the spring that is beside the road to Shur. (Genesis 16:7)

Then the angel of the Lord told her, "Go back to your mistress and submit to her." (Genesis 16:9)

The angel added, "I will so increase your descendants that they will be too numerous to count." (Genesis 16:10)

The angel of the Lord also said to her: "You are now with child and you will have a son. You shall name him Ishmael, for the Lord has heard of your misery. (Genesis 16:11)

God heard the boy crying, and the angel of God called to Hagar from heaven and said to her, "What is the matter, Hagar? Do not be afraid; God has heard the boy crying as he lies there." (Genesis 21:17)

But the angel of the Lord called out to him from heaven, "Abraham! Abraham!" "Here I am," he replied. (Genesis 22:11)

The angel of the LORD called to Abraham from heaven a second time . . . (Genesis 22:15)

"The LORD, the God of heaven, who brought me out of my father's household and my native land and who spoke to me and promised me on oath, saying, 'To your offspring I will give this land'—he will send his angel before you so that you can get a wife for my son from there." (Genesis 24:7)

"He replied, 'The LORD, before whom I have walked, will send his angel with you and make your journey a success, so that you can get a wife for my son from my own clan and from my father's family. . . .' " (Genesis 24:40)

"The angel of God said to me in the dream, 'Jacob.' I answered, 'Here I am.' " (Genesis 31:11)

". . . the angel who has delivered me from all harm—may he bless these boys. May they be called by my name and the names of my fathers Abraham and Isaac, and may they increase greatly upon the earth." (Genesis 48:16)

■   ■   ■   ■   ■

There the angel of the LORD appeared to him in flames of fire from within a bush. Moses saw that though the bush was on fire it did not burn up. (Exodus 3:2)

Then the angel of God, who had been traveling in front of Israel's army, withdrew and went behind them. The pillar of cloud also moved from in front and stood behind them . . . (Exodus 14:19)

"See, I am sending an angel ahead of you to guard you along the way and to bring you to the place I have prepared." (Exodus 23:20)

"My angel will go ahead of you and bring you into the land of the Amorites, Hittites, Perizzites, Canaanites, Hivites and Jebusites, and I will wipe them out." (Exodus 23:23)

"Now go, lead the people to the place I spoke of, and my angel will go before you. However, when the time comes for me to punish, I will punish them for their sin." (Exodus 32:34)

"I will send an angel before you and drive out the Canaanites, Amorites, Hittites, Perizzites, Hivites and Jebusites." (Exodus 33:2)

■   ■   ■   ■   ■

". . . but when we cried out to the LORD, he heard our cry and sent an angel and brought us out of Egypt. Now we are here at Kadesh, a town on the edge of your territory." (Numbers 20:16)

But God was very angry when he went, and the angel of the LORD stood in the road to oppose him. Balaam was riding on his donkey, and his two servants were with him. (Number 22:22)

When the donkey saw the angel of the LORD standing in the road with a drawn sword in his hand, she turned off the road into a field. Balaam beat her to get her back on the road. (Numbers 22:23)

Then the angel of the LORD stood in a narrow path between two vineyards, with walls on both sides. (Numbers 22:24)

When the donkey saw the angel of the LORD, she pressed close to the wall, crushing Balaam's foot against it. So he beat her again. (Numbers 22:25)

Then the angel of the LORD moved on ahead and stood in a narrow place where there was no room to turn, either to the right or to the left. (Numbers 22:26)

When the donkey saw the angel of the LORD, she lay down under Balaam, and he was angry and beat her with his staff. (Numbers 22:27)

Then the LORD opened Balaam's eyes, and he saw the angel of the LORD standing in the road with his sword drawn. So he bowed low and fell facedown. (Numbers 22:31)

The angel of the LORD asked him, "Why have you beaten your donkey these three times? I have come here to oppose you because your path is a reckless one before me." (Numbers 22:32)

Balaam said to the angel of the LORD, "I have sinned. I did not realize you were standing in the road to oppose me. Now if you are displeased, I will go back." (Number 22:34)

The angel of the LORD said to Balaam, "Go with the men, but speak only what I tell you." So Balaam went with the princes of Balak. (Numbers 22:35)

■   ■   ■   ■   ■

The angel of the LORD went up from Gilgal to Bokim and said, "I brought you up out of Egypt and led you into the land that I swore to give to your forefathers. I said, 'I will never break my covenant with you . . .' " (Judges 2:1)

When the angel of the LORD had spoken these things to all the Israelites, the people wept aloud . . . (Judges 2:4)

"Curse Meroz," said the angel of the LORD. "Curse its people bitterly, because they did not come to help the LORD, to help the LORD against the mighty." (Judges 5:23)

The angel of the LORD came and sat down under the oak in Ophrah that belonged to Joash the Abiezrite, where his son Gideon was threshing wheat in a winepress to keep it from the Midianites. (Judges 6:11)

When the angel of the LORD appeared to Gideon, he said, "The LORD is with you, mighty warrior." (Judges 6:12)

The angel of God said to him, "Take the meat and the unleavened bread, place them on this rock, and pour out the broth." And Gideon did so. (Judges 6:20)

With the tip of the staff that was in his hand, the angel of the LORD touched the meat and the unleavened bread. Fire flared from the rock, consuming the meat and the bread. And the angel of the LORD disappeared. (Judges 6:21)

When Gideon realized that it was the angel of the LORD, he exclaimed, "Ah, Sovereign LORD! I have seen the angel of the LORD face to face!" (Judges 6:22)

The angel of the LORD appeared to her and said, "You are sterile and childless, but you are going to conceive and have a son." (Judges 13:3)

Then the woman went to her husband and told him, "A man of God came to me. He looked like an angel of God, very awesome. I didn't ask him where he came from, and he didn't tell me his name." (Judges 13:6)

God heard Manoah, and the angel of God came again to the woman while she was out in the field; but her husband Manoah was not with her. (Judges 13:9)

The angel of the LORD answered, "Your wife must do all that I have told her." (Judges 13:13)

The angel of the LORD replied, "Even though you detain me, I will not eat any of your food. But if you prepare a burnt offering, offer it to the LORD." (Manoah did not realize that it was the angel of the LORD.) (Judges 13:16)

Then Manoah inquired of the angel of the LORD, "What is your name, so that we may honor you when your word comes true?" (Judges 13:17)

As the flame blazed up from the altar toward heaven, the angel of the LORD ascended in the flame. Seeing this, Manoah and his wife fell with their faces to the ground. (Judges 13:20)

When the angel of the LORD did not show himself again to Manoah and his wife, Manoah realized that it was the angel of the LORD.(Judges 13:21)

■ ■ ■ ■ ■

Achish answered, "I know that you have been as pleasing in my eyes as an angel of God; nevertheless, the Philistine commanders have said, 'He must not go up with us into battle.' " (1 Samuel 29:9)

"And now your servant says, 'May the word of my lord the king bring me rest, for my lord the king is like an angel of God in discerning good and evil. May the LORD your God be with you' " (2 Samuel 14:17)

"Your servant Joab did this to change the present situation. My lord has wisdom like that of an angel of God—he knows everything that happens in the land." (2 Samuel 14:20)

". . . And he has slandered your servant to my lord the king. My lord the king is like an angel of God; so do whatever pleases you." (2 Samuel 19:27)

When the angel stretched out his hand to destroy Jerusalem, the LORD was grieved because of the calamity and said to the angel who was afflicting the people, "Enough! Withdraw your hand." The angel of the LORD was then at the threshing floor of Araunah the Jebusite. (2 Samuel 24:16)

When David saw the angel who was striking down the people, he said to the LORD, "I am the one who has sinned and done wrong. These are but sheep. What have they done? Let your hand fall upon me and my family." (2 Samuel 24:17)

■ ■ ■ ■ ■

The old prophet answered, "I too am a prophet, as you are. And an angel said to me by the word of the LORD: 'Bring him back with you to your house so that he may eat bread and drink water.' " (But he was lying to him.) (1 Kings 13:18)

Then he lay down under the tree and fell asleep. All at once an angel touched him and said, "Get up and eat." (1 Kings 19:5)

The angel of the LORD came back a second time and touched him and said, "Get up and eat, for the journey is too much for you." (1 Kings 19:7)

But the angel of the LORD said to Elijah the Tishbite, "Go up and meet the messengers of the king of Samaria and ask them, 'Is it because there is no God in Israel that you are going off to consult Baal-Zebub, the god of Ekron?' " (2 Kings 1:3)

The angel of the LORD said to Elijah, "Go down with him; do not be afraid of him." So Elijah got up and went down with him to the king. (2 Kings 1:15)

That night the angel of the LORD went out and put to death a hundred and eighty-five thousand men in the Assyrian camp. When the people got up the next morning—there were all the dead bodies! (2 Kings 19:35)

■   ■   ■   ■   ■

" '. . . three years of famine, three months of being swept away before your enemies, with their swords overtaking you, or three days of the sword of the LORD—days of plague in the land, with the angel of the LORD ravaging every part of Israel.' Now then, decide how I should answer the one who sent me." (1 Chronicles 21:12)

And God sent an angel to destroy Jerusalem. But as the angel was doing so, the LORD saw it and was grieved because of the calamity and said to the angel who was destroying the people, "Enough! Withdraw your hand." The angel of the LORD was then standing at the threshing floor of Araunah the Jebusite. (1 Chronicles 21:15)

David looked up and saw the angel of the LORD standing between heaven and earth, with a drawn sword in his hand extended over Jerusalem. Then David and the elders, clothed in sackcloth, fell face-down. (1 Chronicles 21:16)

Then the angel of the LORD ordered Gad to tell David to go up and build an altar to the LORD on the threshing floor of Araunah the Jebusite. (1 Chronicles 21:18)

While Araunah was threshing wheat, he turned and saw the angel; his four sons who were with him hid themselves. (1 Chronicles 21:20)

Then the LORD spoke to the angel, and he put his sword back into its sheath. (1 Chronicles 21:27)

But David could not go before it to inquire of God, because he was afraid of the sword of the angel of the LORD.(1 Chronicles 21:30)

And the LORD sent an angel, who annihilated all the fighting men and the leaders and officers in the camp of the Assyrian king. So he withdrew to his own land in disgrace. And when he went into the temple of his god, some of his sons cut him down with the sword. (2 Chronicles 32:21)

■　■　■　■　■

"Yet if there is an angel on his side as a mediator, one out of a thousand, to tell a man what is right for him . . ." (Job 33:23)

■　■　■　■　■

The angel of the LORD encamps around those who fear him, and he delivers them. (Psalm 34:7)

May they be like chaff before the wind, with the angel of the LORD driving them away; (Psalm 35:5)

May their path be dark and slippery, with the angel of the LORD pursuing them. (Psalm 35:6)

■   ■   ■   ■   ■

Then the angel of the LORD went out and put to death a hundred and eighty-five thousand men in the Assyrian camp. When the people got up the next morning—there were all the dead bodies! (Isaiah 37:36)

In all their distress he too was distressed, and the angel of his presence saved them. In his love and mercy he redeemed them; he lifted them up and carried them all the days of old. (Isaiah 63:9)

■   ■   ■   ■   ■

Then Nebuchadnezzar said, "Praise be to the God of Shadrach, Meshach and Abednego, who has sent his angel and rescued his servants! They trusted in him and defied the king's command and were willing to give up their lives rather than serve or worship any god except their own God." (Daniel 3:28)

"My God sent his angel, and he shut the mouths of the lions. They have not hurt me, because I was found innocent in his sight. Nor have I ever done any wrong before you, O king." (Daniel 6:22)

■   ■   ■   ■   ■

He struggled with the angel and overcame him; he wept and begged for his favor. He found him at Bethel and talked with him there . . . (Hosea 12:4)

■   ■   ■   ■   ■

I asked, "What are these, my lord?" The angel who was talking with me answered, "I will show you what they are." (Zechariah 1:9)

And they reported to the angel of the LORD, who was standing among the myrtle trees, "We have gone throughout the earth and found the whole world at rest and in peace." (Zechariah 1:11)

Then the angel of the LORD said, "LORD Almighty, how long will you withhold mercy from Jerusalem and from the towns of Judah, which you have been angry with these seventy years?" (Zechariah 1:12)

So the LORD spoke kind and comforting words to the angel who talked with me. (Zechariah 1:13)

Then the angel who was speaking to me said, "Proclaim this word: This is what the LORD Almighty says: 'I am very jealous for Jerusalem and Zion . . .'" (Zechariah 1:14)

I asked the angel who was speaking to me, "What are these?" He answered me, "These are the horns that scattered Judah, Israel and Jerusalem." (Zechariah 1:19)

Then the angel who was speaking to me left, and another angel came to meet him. . . (Zechariah 2:3)

Then he showed me Joshua the high priest standing before the angel of the LORD, and Satan standing at his right side to accuse him. (Zechariah 3:1)

Now Joshua was dressed in filthy clothes as he stood before the angel. (Zechariah 3:3)

Then angel said to those who were standing before him, "Take off his filthy clothes." Then he said to Joshua, "See, I have taken away your sin, and I will put rich garments on you." (Zechariah 3:4)

Then I said, "Put a clean turban on his head." So they put a clean turban on his head and clothed him, while the angel of the LORD stood by. (Zechariah 3:5)

The angel of the LORD gave this charge to Joshua . . . (Zechariah 3:6)

Then the angel who talked with me returned and wakened me, as a man is wakened from his sleep. (Zechariah 4:1)

I asked the angel who talked with me, "What are these, my lord?" (Zechariah 4:4)

Then I asked the angel, "What are these two olive trees on the right and the left of the lampstand?" (Zechariah 4:11)

Then the angel who was speaking to me came forward and said to me, "Look up and see what this is that is appearing." (Zechariah 5:5)

"Where are they taking the basket?" I asked the angel who was speaking to me. (Zechariah 5:10)

I asked the angel who was speaking to me, "What are these, my lord?" (Zechariah 6:4)

The angel answered me, "These are the four spirits of heaven, going out from standing in the presence of the Lord of the whole world." (Zechariah 6:5)

On that day the LORD will shield those who live in Jerusalem, so that the feeblest among them will be like David, and the house of David will be like God, like the Angel of the LORD going before them. (Zechariah 12:8)

■   ■   ■   ■   ■

But after he had considered this, an angel of the Lord appeared to him in a dream and said, "Joseph son of David, do not be afraid to take Mary home as your wife, because what is conceived in her is from the Holy Spirit. . . ." (Matthew 1:20)

When Joseph woke up, he did what the angel of the Lord had commanded him and took Mary home as his wife. (Matthew 1:24)

When they had gone, an angel of the Lord appeared to Joseph in a dream. "Get up," he said, "take the child and his mother and escape to Egypt. Stay there until I tell you, for Herod is going to search for the child to kill him." (Matthew 2:13)

After Herod died, an angel of the Lord appeared in a dream to Joseph in Egypt . . . (Matthew 2:19)

There was a violent earthquake, for an angel of the Lord came down from heaven and, going to the tomb, rolled back the stone and sat on it. (Matthew 28:2)

The angel said to the women, "Do not be afraid, for I know that you are looking for Jesus, who was crucified . . . ." (Matthew 28:5)

■   ■   ■   ■   ■

Then an angel of the Lord appeared to him, standing at the right side of the altar of incense. (Luke 1:11)

But the angel said to him: "Do not be afraid, Zechariah; your prayer has been heard. Your wife Elizabeth will bear you a son, and you are to give him the name John . . . ." (Luke 1:13)

Zechariah asked the angel, "How can I be sure of this? I am an old man and my wife is well along in years." (Luke 1:18)

The angel answered, "I am Gabriel. I stand in the presence of God, and I have been sent to speak to you and to tell you this good news . . . ." (Luke 1:19)

In the sixth month, God sent the angel Gabriel to Nazareth, a town in Galilee . . . (Luke 1:26)

The angel went to her and said, "Greetings, you who are highly favored! The Lord is with you." (Luke 1:28)

But the angel said to her, "Do not be afraid, Mary, you have found favor with God . . . ." (Luke 1:30)

"How will this be," Mary asked the angel, "since I am a virgin?" (Luke 1:34)

The angel answered, "The Holy Spirit will come upon you, and the power of the Most High will overshadow you. So the holy one to be born will be called the Son of God. . ." (Luke 1:35)

"I am the Lord's servant," Mary answered. "May it be to me as you have said." Then the angel left her. (Luke 1:38)

An angel of the Lord appeared to them, and the glory of the Lord shone around them, and they were terrified. (Luke 2:9)

But the angel said to them, "Do not be afraid. I bring you good news of great joy that will be for all the people. . . ." (Luke 2:10)

Suddenly a great company of the heavenly host appeared with the angel, praising God and saying . . . (Luke 2:13)

On the eighth day, when it was time to circumcise him, he was named Jesus, the name the angel had given him before he had been conceived. (Luke 2:21)

An angel from heaven appeared to him and strengthened him. (Luke 22:43)

■　■　■　■　■

The crowd that was there and heard it said it had thundered; others said an angel had spoken to him. (John 12:29)

■　■　■　■　■

But during the night an angel of the Lord opened the doors of the jail and brought them out. (Acts 5:19)

All who were sitting in the Sanhedrin looked intently at Stephen, and they saw that his face was like the face of an angel. (Acts 6:15)

"After forty years had passed, an angel appeared to Moses in the flames of a burning bush in the desert near Mount Sinai. . . ." (Acts 7:30)

"This is the same Moses whom they had rejected with the words, 'Who made you ruler and judge?' He was sent to be their ruler and delivered by God himself, through the angel who appeared to him in the bush." (Acts 7:35)

"He was in the assembly in the desert, with the angel who spoke to him on Mount Sinai, and with our fathers; and he received living words to pass on to us." (Acts 7:38)

Now an angel of the Lord said to Philip, "Go south to the road—the desert road—that goes down from Jerusalem to Gaza." (Acts 8:26)

One day at about three in the afternoon he had a vision. He distinctly saw an angel of God, who came to him and said, "Cornelius!" (Acts 10:3)

Cornelius stared at him in fear. "What is it, Lord?" he asked. The angel answered, "Your prayers and gifts to the poor have come up as a memorial offering before God. . . ." (Acts 10:4)

When the angel who spoke to him had gone, Cornelius called two of his servants and a devout soldier who was one of his attendants. (Acts 10:7)

The men replied, "We have come from Cornelius the centurion. He is a righteous and God-fearing man, who is respected by all the Jewish people. A holy angel told him to have you come to his house so that he could hear what you have to say." (Acts 10:22)

"He told us how he had seen an angel appear in his house and say, 'Send to Joppa for Simon who is called Peter. . . .' " (Acts 11:13)

Suddenly an angel of the Lord appeared and a light shone in the cell. He struck Peter on the side and woke him up. "Quick, get up!" he said, and the chains fell off Peter's wrists. (Acts 12:7)

Then the angel said to him, "Put on your clothes and sandals." And Peter did so. "Wrap your cloak around you and follow me," the angel told him. (Acts 12:8)

Peter followed him out of the prison, but he had no idea that what the angel was doing was really happening; he thought he was seeing a vision. (Acts 12:9)

They passed the first and second guards and came to the iron gate leading to the city. It opened for them by itself, and they went through it. When they had walked the length of one street, suddenly the angel left him. (Acts 12:10)

Then Peter came to himself and said, "Now I know without a doubt that the Lord sent his angel and rescued me from Herod's clutches and from everything the Jewish people were anticipating." (Acts 12:11)

"You're out of your mind," they told her. When she kept insisting that it was so, they said, "It must be his angel." (Acts 12:15)

Immediately, because Herod did not give praise to God, an angel of the Lord struck him down, and he was eaten by worms and died. (Acts 12:23)

There was a great uproar, and some of the teachers of the law who were Pharisees stood up and argued vigorously. "We find nothing wrong with this man," they said. "What if a spirit or an angel has spoken to him?" (Acts 23:9)

Last night an angel of the God whose I am and whom I serve stood beside me . . . (Acts 27:23)

■   ■   ■   ■   ■

And do not grumble, as some of them did—and were killed by the destroying angel. (1 Corinthians 10:10)

And no wonder, for Satan himself masquerades as an angel of light. (2 Corinthians 11:14)

■   ■   ■   ■   ■

But even if we or an angel from heaven should preach a gospel other than the one we preached to you, let him be eternally condemned! (Galatians 1:8)

Even though my illness was a trial to you, you did not treat me with contempt or scorn. Instead, you welcomed me as if I were an angel of God, as if I were Christ Jesus himself. (Galatians 4:14)

■   ■   ■   ■   ■

The revelation of Jesus Christ, which God gave him to show his servants what must soon take place. He made it known by sending his angel to his servant John . . . (Revelation 1:1)

"To the angel of the church in Ephesus write: These are the words of him who holds the seven stars in his right hand and walks among the seven golden lampstands: . . ." (Revelation 2:1)

"To the angel of the church in Smyrna write: These are the words of him who is the First and the Last, who died and came to life again. . ." (Revelation 2:8)

"To the angel of the church in Pergamum write: These are the words of him who has the sharp, double-edged sword. . ." (Revelation 2:12)

"To the angel of the church in Thyatira write: These are the words of the Son of God, whose eyes are like blazing fire and whose feet are like burnished bronze. . . ." (Revelation 2:18)

"To the angel of the church in Sardis write: These are the words of him who holds the seven spirits of God and the seven stars. I know your deeds; you have a reputation of being alive, but you are dead. . . ." (Revelation 3:1)

"To the angel of the church in Philadelphia write: These are the words of him who is holy and true, who holds the key of David. What he opens no one can shut, and what he shuts no one can open. . . ." (Revelation 3:7)

"To the angel of the church in Laodicea write: These are the words of the Amen, the faithful and true witness, the ruler of God's creation. . . ." (Revelation 3:14)

And I saw a mighty angel proclaiming in a loud voice, "Who is worthy to break the seals and open the scroll?" (Revelation 5:2)

Then I saw another angel coming up from the east, having the seal of the living God. He called out in a loud voice to the four angels who had been given power to harm the land and the sea . . . (Revelation 7:2)

Another angel, who had a golden censer, came and stood at the altar. He was given much incense to offer, with the prayers of all the saints, on the golden altar before the throne. (Revelation 8:3)

Then the angel took the censer, filled it with fire from the altar, and hurled it on the earth; and there came peals of thunder, rumblings, flashes of lightning and an earthquake. (Revelation 8:5)

The first angel sounded his trumpet, and there came hail and fire mixed with blood, and it was hurled down upon the earth. A third of the earth was burned up, a third of the trees were burned up, and all the green grass was burned up. (Revelation 8:7)

The second angel sounded his trumpet, and something like a huge mountain, all ablaze, was thrown into the sea. A third of the sea turned into blood . . . (Revelation 8:8)

The third angel sounded his trumpet, and a great star, blazing like a torch, fell from the sky on a third of the rivers and on the springs of water. . . (Revelation 8:10)

The fourth angel sounded his trumpet, and a third of the sun was struck, a third of the moon, and a third of the stars, so that a third of them turned dark. A third of the day was without light, and also a third of the night. (Revelation 8:12)

The fifth angel sounded his trumpet, and I saw a star that had fallen from the sky to the earth. The star was given the key to the shaft of the Abyss. (Revelation 9:1)

They had as king over them the angel of the Abyss, whose name in Hebrew is Abaddon, and in Greek, Apollyon. (Revelation 9:11)

The sixth angel sounded his trumpet, and I heard a voice coming from the horns of the golden altar that is before God. (Revelation 9:13)

It said to the sixth angel who had the trumpet, "Release the four angels who are bound at the great river Euphrates." (Revelation 9:14)

Then I saw another mighty angel coming down from heaven. He was robed in a cloud, with a rainbow above his head; his face was like the sun, and his legs were like fiery pillars. (Revelation 10:1)

Then the angel I had seen standing on the sea and on the land raised his right hand to heaven. (Revelation 10:5)

". . . but in the days when the seventh angel is about to sound his trumpet, the mystery of God will be accomplished, just as he announced to his servants the prophets." (Revelation 10:7)

Then the voice that I had heard from heaven spoke to me once more: "Go, take the scroll that lies open in the hand of the angel who is standing on the sea and on the land." (Revelation 10:8)

So I went to the angel and asked him to give me the little scroll. He said to me, "Take it and eat it. It will turn your stomach sour, but in your mouth it will be as sweet as honey." (Revelation 10:9)

The seventh angel sounded his trumpet, and there were loud voices in heaven, which said: "The kingdom of the world has become the kingdom of our Lord and of his Christ, and he will reign for ever and ever." (Revelation 11:15)

Then I saw another angel flying in midair, and he had the eternal gospel to proclaim to those who live on the earth—to every nation, tribe, language and people. (Revelation 14:6)

A second angel followed and said, "Fallen! Fallen is Babylon the Great, which made all the nations drink the maddening wine of her adulteries." (Revelation 14:8)

A third angel followed them and said in a loud voice: "If anyone worships the beast and his image and receives his mark on the forehead or on the hand . . ." (Revelation 14:9)

Then another angel came out of the temple and called in a loud voice to him who was sitting on the cloud, "Take your sickle and reap, because the time to reap has come, for the harvest of the earth is ripe." (Revelation 14:15)

Another angel came out of the temple in heaven, and he too had a sharp sickle. (Revelation 14:17)

Still another angel, who had charge of the fire, came from the altar and called in a loud voice to him who had the sharp sickle, "Take your sharp sickle and gather the clusters of grapes from the earth's vine, because its grapes are ripe." (Revelation 14:18)

The angel swung his sickle on the earth, gathered its grapes and threw them into the great winepress of God's wrath. (Revelation 14:19)

The first angel went and poured out his bowl on the land, and ugly and painful sores broke out on the people who had the mark of the beast and worshiped his image. (Revelation 16:2)

The second angel poured out his bowl on the sea, and it turned into blood like that of a dead man, and every living thing in the sea died. (Revelation 16:3)

The third angel poured out his bowl on the rivers and springs of water, and they became blood. (Revelation 16:4)

Then I heard the angel in charge of the waters say: "You are just in these judgments, you who are and who were, the Holy One, because you have so judged; . . ." (Revelation 16:5)

The fourth angel poured out his bowl on the sun, and the sun was given power to scorch people with fire. (Revelation 16:8)

The fifth angel poured out his bowl on the throne of the beast, and his kingdom was plunged into darkness. Men gnawed their tongues in agony . . . (Revelation 16:10)

The sixth angel poured out his bowl on the great river Euphrates, and its water was dried up to prepare the way for the kings from the East. (Revelation 16:12)

The seventh angel poured out his bowl into the air, and out of the temple came a loud voice from the throne, saying, "It is done!" (Revelation 16:17)

Then the angel carried me away in the Spirit into a desert. There I saw a woman sitting on a scarlet beast that was covered with blasphemous names and had seven heads and ten horns. (Revelation 17:3)

Then the angel said to me: "Why are you astonished? I will explain to you the mystery of the woman and of the beast she rides, which has the seven heads and ten horns. . . ." (Revelation 17:7)

Then the angel said to me, "The waters you saw, where the prostitute sits, are peoples, multitudes, nations and languages. . . ." (Revelation 17:15)

After this I saw another angel coming down from heaven. He had great authority, and the earth was illuminated by his splendor. (Revelation 18:1)

Then a mighty angel picked up a boulder the size of a large millstone and threw it into the sea, and said: "With such violence the great city of Babylon will be thrown down, never to be found again. . . ." (Revelation 18:21)

Then the angel said to me, "Write: 'Blessed are those who are invited to the wedding supper of the Lamb!'" And he added, "These are the true words of God." (Revelation 19:9)

And I saw an angel standing in the sun, who cried in a loud voice to all the birds flying in midair, "Come, gather together for the great supper of God . . ." (Revelation 19:17)

And I saw an angel coming down out of heaven, having the key to the Abyss and holding in his hand a great chain. (Revelation 20:1)

The angel who talked with me had a measuring rod of gold to measure the city, its gates and its walls. (Revelation 21:15)

He measured its wall and it was 144 cubits thick, by man's measurement, which the angel was using. (Revelation 21:17)

Then the angel showed me the river of the water of life, as clear as crystal, flowing from the throne of God and of the Lamb . . . (Revelation 22:1)

The angel said to me, "These words are trustworthy and true. The Lord, the God of the spirits of the prophets, sent his angel to show his servants the things that must soon take place." (Revelation 22:6)

I, John, am the one who heard and saw these things. And when I had heard and seen them, I fell down at the feet of the angel who had been showing them to me. (Revelation 22:8)

"I, Jesus, have sent my angel to give you this testimony for the churches. I am the Root and the Offspring of David, and the bright Morning Star." (Revelation 22:16)

Bible References to Two or More Angels (96)

The two angels arrived at Sodom in the evening, and Lot was sitting in the gateway of the city. When he saw them, he got up to meet them and bowed down with his face to the ground. (Genesis 19:1)

With the coming of dawn, the angels urged Lot, saying, "Hurry! Take your wife and your two daughters who are here, or you will be swept away when the city is punished." (Genesis 19:15)

He had a dream in which he saw a stairway resting on the earth, with its top reaching to heaven, and the angels of God were ascending and descending on it. (Genesis 28:12)

Jacob also went on his way, and the angels of God met him. (Genesis 32:1)

■ ■ ■ ■ ■

One day the angels came to present themselves before the LORD, and Satan also came with them. (Job 1:6)

On another day the angels came to present themselves before the LORD, and Satan also came with them to present himself before him. (Job 2:1)

"If God places no trust in his servants, if he charges his angels with error . . ." (Job 4:18)

". . . while the morning stars sang together and all the angels shouted for joy?" (Job 38:7)

■   ■   ■   ■   ■

Men ate the bread of angels; he sent them all the food they could eat. (Psalm 78:25)

He unleashed against them his hot anger, his wrath, indignation and hostility—a band of destroying angels. (Psalm 78:49)

For he will command his angels concerning you to guard you in all your ways . . . (Psalm 91:11)

Praise the LORD, you his angels, you mighty ones who do his bidding, who obey his word. (Psalm 103:20)

Praise him, all his angels, praise him, all his heavenly hosts. (Psalm 148:2)

■   ■   ■   ■   ■

"If you are the Son of God," he said, "throw yourself down. For it is written: 'He will command his angels concerning you, and they will lift you up in their hands, so that you will not strike your foot against a stone.' " (Matthew 4:6)

Then the devil left him, and angels came and attended him. (Matthew 4:11)

"... and the enemy who sows them is the devil. The harvest is the end of the age, and the harvesters are angels." (Matthew 13:39)

"The Son of Man will send out his angels, and they will weed out of his kingdom everything that causes sin and all who do evil." (Matthew 13:41)

"This is how it will be at the end of the age. The angels will come and separate the wicked from the righteous ..." (Matthew 13:49)

"For the Son of Man is going to come in his Father's glory with his angels, and then he will reward each person according to what he has done." (Matthew 16:27)

"See that you do not look down on one of these little ones. For I tell you that their angels in heaven always see the face of my Father in heaven." (Matthew 18:10)

"At the resurrection people will neither marry nor be given in marriage; they will be like the angels in heaven." (Matthew 22:30)

"And he will send his angels with a loud trumpet call, and they will gather his elect from the four winds, from one end of the heavens to the other." (Matthew 24:31)

"No one knows about that day or hour, not even the angels in heaven, nor the Son, but only the Father." (Matthew 24:36)

"When the Son of Man comes in his glory, and all the angels with him, he will sit on his throne in heavenly glory." (Matthew 25:31)

"Then he say to those on his left, 'Depart from me, you who are cursed, into the eternal fire prepared for the devil and his angels.'" (Matthew 25:41)

"Do you think I cannot call on my Father, and he will at once put at my disposal more than twelve legions of angels?" (Matthew 26:53)

■   ■   ■   ■   ■

. . . and he was in the desert forty days, being tempted by Satan. He was with the wild animals, and angels attended him. (Mark 1:13)

"If anyone is ashamed of me and my words in this adulterous and sinful generation, the Son of Man will be ashamed of him when he comes in his Father's glory with the holy angels." (Mark 8:38)

"When the dead rise, they will neither marry nor be given in marriage; they will be like the angels in heaven." (Mark 12:25)

"And he will send his angels and gather his elect from the four winds, from the ends of the earth to the ends of the heavens." (Mark 13:27)

"No one knows about that day or hour, not even the angels in heaven, nor the Son, but only the Father." (Mark 13:32)

■   ■   ■   ■   ■

When the angels had left them and gone into heaven, the shepherds said to one another, "Let's go to Bethlehem and see this thing that has happened, which the Lord has told us about." (Luke 2:15)

For it is written: "He will command his angels concerning you to guard you carefully; . . ." (Luke 4:10)

"If anyone is ashamed of me and my words, the Son of Man will be ashamed of him when he comes in his glory and in the glory of the Father and of the holy angels." (Luke 9:26)

"I tell you, whoever acknowledges me before men, the Son of Man will also acknowledge him before the angels of God." (Luke 12:8)

"But he who disowns me before men will be disowned before the angels of God." (Luke 12:9)

"In the same way, I tell you, there is rejoicing in the presence of the angels of God over one sinner who repents." (Luke 15:10)

"The time came when the beggar died and the angels carried him to Abraham's side. The rich man also died and was buried." (Luke 16:22)

". . . and they can no longer die; for they are like the angels. They are God's children, since they are children of the resurrection." (Luke 20:36)

". . . but didn't find his body. They came and told us that they had seen a vision of angels, who said he was alive." (Luke 24:23)

■ ■ ■ ■ ■

He then added, "I tell you the truth, you shall see heaven open, and the angels of God ascending and descending on the Son of Man." (John 1:51)

. . . and saw two angels in white, seated where Jesus' body had been, one at the head and the other at the foot. (John 20:12)

■ ■ ■ ■ ■

". . . you who have received the law that was put into effect through angels but have not obeyed it." (Acts 7:53)

(The Sadducees say that there is no resurrection, and that there are neither angels nor spirits, but the Pharisees acknowledge them all.) (Acts 23:8)

■ ■ ■ ■ ■

For I am convinced that neither death nor life, neither angels nor demons, neither the present nor the future, nor any powers . . . (Romans 8:38)

■   ■   ■   ■   ■

For it seems to me that God has put us apostles on display at the end of the procession, like men condemned to die in the arena. We have been made a spectacle to the whole universe, to angels as well as to men. (1 Corinthians 4:9)

Do you not know that we will judge angels? How much more the things of this life! (1 Corinthians 6:3)

For this reason, and because of the angels, the woman ought to have a sign of authority on her head. (1 Corinthians 11:10)

If I speak in the tongues of men and of angels, but have not love, I am only a resounding gong or a clanging cymbal. (1 Corinthians 13:1)

■   ■   ■   ■   ■

What, then, was the purpose of the law? It was added because of transgressions until the Seed to whom the promise referred had come. The law was put into effect through angels by a mediator. (Galatians 3:19)

■   ■   ■   ■   ■

Do not let anyone who delights in false humility and the worship of angels disqualify you for the prize. Such a person goes into great detail about what he has seen, and his unspiritual mind puffs him up with idle notions. (Colossians 2:18)

■   ■   ■   ■   ■

. . . and give relief to you who are troubled, and to us as well. This will happen when the Lord Jesus is revealed from heaven in blazing fire with his powerful angels. (2 Thessalonians 1:7)

■   ■   ■   ■   ■

Beyond all question, the mystery of godliness is great: He appeared in a body, was vindicated by the Spirit, was seen by angels, was preached among the nations, was believed on in the world, was taken up in glory. (1 Timothy 3:16)

I charge you, in the sight of God and Christ Jesus and the elect angels, to keep these instructions without partiality, and to do nothing out of favoritism. (1 Timothy 5:21)

■   ■   ■   ■   ■

So he became as much superior to the angels as the name he has inherited is superior to theirs. (Hebrews 1:4)

For to which of the angels did God every say, "You are my Son; today I have become your Father"? Or again, "I will be his Father, and he will be my Son"? (Hebrews 1:5)

And again, when God brings his firstborn into the world, he says, "Let all God's angels worship him." (Hebrews 1:6)

In speaking of the angels he says, "He makes his angels winds, his servants flames of fire." (Hebrews 1:7)

To which of the angels did God every say, "Sit at my right hand until I make your enemies a footstool for your feet"? (Hebrews 1:13)

Are not all angels ministering spirits sent to serve those who will inherit salvation? (Hebrews 1:14)

For if the message spoken by angels was binding, and every violation and disobedience received its just punishment . . . (Hebrews 2:2)

It is not to angels that he has subjected the world to come, about which we are speaking. (Hebrews 2:5)

You made him a little lower than the angels; you crowned him with glory and honor . . . (Hebrews 2:7)

but we see Jesus, who was made a little lower than the angels, now crowned with glory and honor because he suffered death, so that by the grace of God he might taste death for everyone. (Hebrews 2:9)

For surely it is not angels he helps, but Abraham's descendants. (Hebrews 2:16)

But you have come to Mount Zion, to the heavenly Jerusalem, the city of the living God. You have come to thousands upon thousands of angels in joyful assembly . . . (Hebrews 12:22)

Do not forget to entertain strangers, for by so doing some people have entertained angels without knowing it. (Hebrews 13:2)

■   ■   ■   ■   ■

It was revealed to them that they were not serving themselves but you, when they spoke of the things that have now been told you by those who have preached the gospel to you by the Holy Spirit sent from heaven. Even angels long to look into these things. (1 Peter 1:12)

. . . who has gone into heaven and is at God's right hand—with angels, authorities and powers in submission to him. (1 Peter 3:22)

■   ■   ■   ■   ■

For if God did not spare angels when they sinned, but sent them to hell, putting them into gloomy dungeons to be held for judgment . . . (2 Peter 2:4)

. . . yet even angels, although they are stronger and more powerful, do not bring slanderous accusations against such beings in the presence of the Lord. (2 Peter 2:11)

■   ■   ■   ■   ■

And the angels who did not keep their positions of authority but abandoned their own home—these he has kept in darkness, bound with everlasting chains for judgment on the great Day. (Jude 1:6)

■   ■   ■   ■   ■

"The mystery of the seven stars that you saw in my right hand and of the seven golden lampstands is this: The seven stars are the angels of the seven churches, and the seven lampstands are the seven churches." (Revelation 1:20)

"He who overcomes will, like them, be dressed in white. I will never blot out his name from the book of life, but will acknowledge his name before my Father and his angels." (Revelation 3:5)

Then I looked and heard the voice of many angels, numbering thousands upon thousands, and ten thousand times ten thousand. They encircled the throne and the living creatures and the elders. (Revelation 5:11)

After this I saw four angels standing at the four corners of the earth, holding back the four winds of the earth to prevent any wind from blowing on the land or on the sea or on any tree. (Revelation 7:1)

Then I saw another angel coming up from the east, having the seal of the living God. He called out in a loud voice to the four angels who had been given power to harm the land and the sea . . . (Revelation 7:2)

All the angels were standing around the throne and around the elders and the four living creatures. They fell down on their faces before the throne and worshiped God . . . (Revelation 7:11)

And I saw the seven angels who stand before God, and to them were given seven trumpets. (Revelation 8:2)

Then the seven angels who had the seven trumpets prepared to sound them. (Revelation 8:6)

As I watched, I heard an eagle that was flying in midair call out in a loud voice: "Woe! Woe! Woe to the inhabitants of the earth, because of the trumpet blasts about to be sounded by the other three angels!" (Revelation 8:13)

It said to the sixth angel who had the trumpet, "Release the four angels who are bound at the great river Euphrates." (Revelation 9:14)

And the four angels who had been kept ready for this very hour and day and month and year were released to kill a third of mankind. (Revelation 9:15)

And there was war in heaven. Michael and his angels fought against the dragon, and the dragon and his angels fought back. (Revelation 12:7)

The great dragon was hurled down—that ancient serpent called the devil, or Satan, who leads the whole world astray. He was hurled to the earth, and his angels with him. (Revelation 12:9)

. . . he, too, will drink of the wine of God's fury, which has been poured full strength into the cup of his wrath. He will be tormented with burning sulfur in the presence of the holy angels and of the Lamb. (Revelation 14:10)

I saw in heaven another great and marvelous sign: seven angels with the seven last plagues—last, because with them God's wrath is completed. (Revelation 15:1)

Out of the temple came the seven angels with the seven plagues. They were dressed in clean, shining linen and wore golden sashes around their chests. (Revelation 15:6)

Then one of the four living creatures gave to the seven angels seven golden bowls filled with the wrath of God, who lives for ever and ever. (Revelation 15:7)

And the temple was filled with smoke from the glory of God and from his power, and no one could enter the temple until the seven plagues of the seven angels were completed. (Revelation 15:8)

Then I heard a loud voice from the temple saying to the seven angels, "Go, pour out the seven bowls of God's wrath on the earth." (Revelation 16:1)

One of the seven angels who had the seven bowls came and said to me, "Come, I will show you the punishment of the great prostitute, who sits on many waters." (Revelation 17:1)

One of the seven angels who had the seven bowls full of the seven last plagues came and said to me, "Come, I will show you the bride, the wife of the Lamb." (Revelation 21:9)

It had a great, high wall with twelve gates, and with twelve angels at the gates. On the gates were written the names of the twelve tribes of Israel. (Revelation 21:12)

What Others over the Centuries Have Written About Angels

If then we love angels, let us be sober, as though we were in the presence of tutors, for there is a demon present also.

—*John Chrysostom* (350–405)

To the heavenly Angels, who possess God in humility and serve Him with blessedness, to whom all material, nations and all rational life are subject. Every visible thing in this world is put in charge of Angels. Angels are spirits, but it is not because they are Angels that they are Angels. They are Angels because they are sent, for the name Angel refers to their office not to their nature. In as far as he exists, an Angel is spirit, in as far as he acts, he is an Angel.

—*St. Augustine* (354–430)

Man lives in the middle of a supernatural world—everything that seems empty is filled with the angels of God, and there is no place that is not inhabited by them. Angels do not only protect the soul, they continue throughout the whole course of our lives to protect us from the attacks of the Devil, and to participate in the progress of our lives.

—*St. Hilary of Poitier* (315–368)

The Most High has commanded the Angels, his Angels—his closest friends. He has given his Angels charge over you. Who are you? . . .

what do you think he has ordered them to do for your sake? . . . To protect you.

—*St. Bernard of Clairvaux* (1090–1153)

Angels are spiritual creatures, created by God, without a body for the service of Christendom and the Church.

—*Martin Luther* (1483–1546)

Angels are the dispensers and the administrators of the Divine beneficence towards us; they regard our safety, undertake our defense, direct our ways and exercise a constant solicitude that no evil befall us . . . God does not make angels the ministers of His power and goodness in order to divide His glory with them, so neither does He promise His assistance in their ministry, that *we* may divide our confidence between them and Him.

—*John Calvin*
(*Institutes of Religion,* Book 1, Chapter 4, 1536)

The offices given by God to Angels, the great works done by them, the excellent gifts wherewith they are endued knowledge, wisdom, holiness and strength do plainly demonstrate they are true real substances. The properties of Angels are many; the excellent ones are knowledge, prudence, purity, glory, power, speed, zeal and constancy.

—*William Gouge*
(*Hebrews,* 1578–1653)

Millions of spiritual creatures walk the earth when we sleep and when we wake.

—*John Milton* (1608–1674)

Angels are unseen attendants of the saints of God: they bear us up in their hands lest we dash our foot against a stone. Loyalty to their Lord leads them to take a deep interest in the children of His love. They rejoice over the return of the prodigal to his father's house, and they welcome the advent of the believer to the King's palace above.

—*C. H. Spurgeon* (1834–1892)

In many respects Angels may have been made inferior even to man as he came out of the Lord his Maker, for he was made in the *"likeness of God;"* but of the Angels, even the highest order of them, this is never spoken.

—*Adam Clarke*
(Commentary on Hebrews, 1837)

Angels have manifested themselves to men and women through vision, hearing and feeling. Why then should we consider them purely immortal substance having no connection with the visible universe? Our knowledge of Angels leads us to believe they are connected with the world of matter.

—*Thomas Timpson*
(Angel of God, 1845)

With silence only as their benediction, God's Angels come, where, in the shadow of a great affliction, the souls sit dumb.

—*John Greenleaf Whittier* (1807–1892)

The Angels are attendant servants of God, created to do His will, accompany Him as the clouds and lightning do. They are prompt to do His will, rapid, quick and obedient in His service.

—*Albert Barnes*
(Epistle to Hebrews, 1868)

Angels, being like ourselves personal, find special interest in what has character of its own. They sympathize strongly with individual life, and can discern what is distinctive, when to the unpurged eye each specimen seems like the rest . . . Sheep, to the Londoner, seem all alike, but the shepherd knows the face of every one of his flock.

—*Henry Latham*
(Service of Angels, 1894)

The ministry of Angels may be divided into two parts, that of praising God, and the execution of His behests.

—*Alfred Edersheim*
(Life and Times of Jesus the Messiah, 1890)

While we struggle in His name against sin, and relying on His help to overcome, we are surrounded by invisible forms who watch with interest, and who are near in times of peril, weakness and doubt, to shield us from change and to strengthen and support. They may call to mind some passage from God's Word, thus lightening the inner man or woman by refreshing and invigorating the very spring of hidden life.

—*Charles Bell*
(*Angel Beings,* 1878)

Jacob went on his way and the Angel of God met him. He was no longer a romantic youth, he was now an unromantic wayfarer. The way was hard and dusty, there was none of the mystery of Bethel. Yet the angel who strove at Bethel came back again onto the common road where his feet were plodding along wearily. We ought all to have an experience like Jacob. . . . Life will never be the same if we have seen the angels.

—*G. H. Morrison*
(*Return of the Angels,* 1909)

Probably the most persistent sentiment with me is the watch of angel hosts in answer to the prayers of the numerous saints in the homeland. It seems to me as if this special watch of angels surround this boat, I seem to hear them in the rolling air and to feel their touches even through my whole body.

—*Oswald Chambers*
(from his letter to his mother aboard *S. S. Baltic*
on his way to Japan, 1906)

Angels are persons, they are spirits, they have a body corresponding to their spiritual nature. Their dwelling places are in the heavenlies; the stars are in the heavens. Where else can we locate the habitation of angels, but among the stars?

—*A. C. Gaebelein* (1861–1945)

The ministry of watcher-angels, their conflicts with strong resistance in heavenly graces, their interest in our strifes and tears and prayers, one dwelt upon at length, expanded and expounded until we see their forms in rainbows and suns, and hear their trumpets sounding from star to star, and hear their resonant voices as they call to each other in their patrol through the worlds.

—*F. B. Meyer*
(From his comments on the Book of Revelation, 1911)

Angels are only servants of God and man—they are essentially marginal figures.

—*Karl Barth* (1886–1968)

The truth that there is an order of celestial beings quite distinct from humanity and from the Godhead who occupy an exalted estate above the present position of man is the teaching of much of scripture. . . . The faithful service of Angels to mankind cannot be explained on the grounds of their love for humanity. They are interested in that which concerns their God. . . . The Angels are servants of man in a thousand ways.

—*Lewis Sperry Chafer*
(*Systematic Theology*, 1947)

The denial of the existence of Angels springs from the materialistic and unbelieving spirit, which in its most terrible form denies the existence of God.

—*Merril Unger*
(*Bible Dictionary*, 1957)

I am convinced that these heavenly beings exist and that they provide unseen aid on our behalf. I also believe in Angels because I have sensed their presence in my life on special occasions. . . . When the Christians die, an Angel will be there to comfort us, to give us peace and joy at that most critical hour and usher us into the presence of God whom we shall dwell with, the Lord forever.

—*Billy Graham*
(*Angels*, 1975)

The Angel is one of those Articles of Faith as unshaken as our belief in the existence of God.

—*Malcolm Goodwin*
(*Angels*, 1990)

Of course, some people will say Angels don't exist, never having seen one. And other people will ask why they appear only to certain humans. Others will say that Angels come to everyone. The question is who will recognize them when they come?

—*Sophy Burnham*
(*A Book of Angels,* 1992)

Angels are creations of God, and under the direction of the Holy Spirit they help us carry out our assignments as believers.

—*Terry Law*
(*The Truth about Angels,* 1994)

Angels, then, are real. Angels are spiritual beings, godlike but not God. Nor are they human—though they may appear in human form—they are immortal.

—*Larry Kinnaman*
(*Angels Light and Dark,* 1994)

Bibliography

Adler, Mortimer. *The Angels and Us.* New York: Collier Books, 1993.

Anderson, Joan Webster. *Where Angels Walk.* New York: Guideposts, 1992.

Bell, Charles. *Angelic Beings, Their Nature and Ministry.* London: Religious Tract Society, 1875.

Bubeck, Mark I. *The Adversary.* California: Here's Life, 1975.

_____. *The Satanic Revival.* California: Here's Life, 1991.

Card, Wesley. *Angels and Principalities.* Cambridge, England: Cambridge University Press, 1972.

Conner, John. *Do You Have a Guardian Angel?* Murfreesboro: Mamre Press, 1985.

Connolly, David. *In Search of Angels.* New York: Perigee Books, 1993.

Daniel, Ramer, Wyllie. *Ask Your Angels.* New York: Ballantine, 1992.

Danielou, Jean. *Angels, their Mission.* Westminster, Maryland: Christian Classics, (n.d.).

Ferves, Timothy. *Galaxies.* New York: Harrison House, 1987.

Gaebelein, A. C. *Angels.* Grand Rapids: Baker Book House, 1987.

Goodwin, Malcolm. *Angels, An Endangered Species.* New York: Simon & Schuster, 1990.

Graham, Billy. *Angels: God's Secret Agents.* New York: Doubleday, 1975.

Kinnaman, Gary. *Angels Dark and Light.* Ann Arbor, Michigan: Servant Publications, 1994.

Kraft, Charles H. *Defeating Dark Angels.* Ann Arbor, Michigan: Servant Publications, 1992.

Langton, Edward. *The Angel Teachings of the New Testament.* London: James Clarke & Company, (n.d).

Latham, Henry. *A Service of Angels*. Cambridge, England: Deighton Bell, 1896.

Law, Terry. *The Truth about Angels*. Altamonte Springs, Florida: Creation House, 1994.

Lindsey, Hal. *Satan Alive and Well*. Grand Rapids, Michigan: Zondervan Publishing House, 1972.

Lockyer, Herbert, Sr. *Satan, His Person and Power*. Dallas, Texas: Word Publishing, 1980.

Lucado, Max. *And the Angels were Silent*. Portland: Multnomah Press, 1992.

Morrison, G. H. *The Return of Angels*. London: Hodder & Stoughton, 1909.

Northrup, L. W. *Encounter with Angels*. Wheaton: Tyndale House, 1988.

Peterson's Guide to the Stars. Boston: Houghton Mifflin, 1983.

Rhodes, Ron. *Angels Among Us*. Eugene, Oregon: Harvest House, 1994.

Shaw, Gwen. *Our Ministering Angels*. Arkansas: Engeltal Press, 1986.

Shedd, Charlie. *Brush of an Angel's Wing*. Ann Arbor, Michigan: Servant Publications, 1994.

Snell, Joy. *The Ministry of Angels*. London: Greater World Association, 1918.

Stier, Rudolph. *The Words of Angels*. London: Swan Lowrey, 1886.

Strauss, Lehman. *Thank God for Good Angels*. Neptune, New Jersey: Loizeaux Brothers, 1976.

Taylor, Terry Lynn. *Messengers of Light*. Tiburon, California: H. J. Kramer, Inc., 1990.

Timpson, Thomas. *The Angels of God*. London: John Snow, 1845.

Reference Material

Barnes, Albert. *Epistle to the Hebrews*. New York: Harper, 1868.

Berkhof, Louis. *Manual of Christian Doctrine*. Grand Rapids: Eerdmans, 1983.

Calvin, John. *Institutes of the Christian Religion*. Philadelphia, Pennsylvania: Westminster Press, 1867.

Chafer, Lewis Sperry. *Systematic Theology*. Dallas, Texas: Dallas Seminary, 1948.

Clarke, Adam. *Commentary on the Whole Bible.* New York: Mason & Lane, 1837.

Ellicott's Commentary on the Whole Bible. Grand Rapids: Zondervan, 1954.

Encyclopedia Judaica. Jerusalem: Keter Publishers, 1972.

Frowde, Henry. *Companion Bible.* London: Oxford University Press, (n.d.).

George, William. *Commentary on Hebrews.* Grand Rapids, Michigan: Kregel, 1980.

Gill, Dr. J. *Body of Divinity.* (n.p., n.d.).

Hodge, Charles. *Systematic Theology.* New York: Charles Scribner & Sons, 1895.

Matthew Henry's Commentary. Peabody, Mass.: Hendrickson Publishers, 1991.

Morgan, Dr. G. Campbell. *Revelation of John.* London: Pickering & Inglis, Ltd., 1915.

New Catholic Encyclopedia. Washington, D.C.: Catholic University of America, 1967.

Newberry, Thomas. *Newberry Study Bible.* Grand Rapids, Michigan: Kregel, 1960.

Owen, John. *Commentary on Hebrews.* Grand Rapids: Kregel, 1979.

Phillips, J. B. *The Book of Revelation.* New York: Macmillian Company, 1958.

Phillips, J. B. *The New Testament in Modern English.* London: Geoffrey Bles, 1960.

Schaffer-Herzog. *Herzog Encyclopedia of Religious Knowledge.* New York: Funk & Wagnalls, 1908.

Young's Concordance. Peabody, Mass.: Hendrickson Publishers, 1984.